ON OBSESSION

A CLINICAL AND METHODOLOGICAL STUDY

NERVOUS AND MENTAL DISEASE MONOGRAPHS

[No. 73]

ON OBSESSION

A Clinical and Methodological Study

By

ERWIN W. STRAUS

DIRECTOR OF PROFESSIONAL EDUCATION AND RESEARCH
U. S. VETERANS ADMINISTRATION HOSPITAL
LEXINGTON, KY.

LECTURER IN PSYCHOLOGY, UNIVERSITY OF KENTUCKY
LEXINGTON, KY.

CLINICAL ASSOCIATE IN PSYCHIATRY, UNIVERSITY
OF LOUISVILLE MEDICAL SCHOOL
LOUISVILLE, KY.

1948

NERVOUS AND MENTAL DISEASE MONOGRAPHS
NEW YORK

Reprinted with the permission of the original publisher

JOHNSON REPRINT CORPORATION
111 Fifth Avenue, New York, N.Y. 10003

JOHNSON REPRINT COMPANY LTD.
Berkeley Square House, London, W. 1

This study, performed at The Johns Hopkins University, Baltimore, was made possible through a grant of the National Committee for Mental Hygiene for Research on Dementia Praecox on funds supplied by the Scottish Rite Masons, 1944-1945 and 1945-1946

First reprinting, 1968, Johnson Reprint Corporation

Printed in the United States of America

PREFACE

PSYCHOSES AND NEUROSES are variations of human experience and behavior. They are, as it has been said, experiments, arranged by nature herself. If this were so, the psychiatric wards might be seen as the great, natural laboratories of psychology. But there is a marked contrast between these experiments of nature and the usual conditions of scientific research. The physicist in his laboratory chooses a well known situation for his point of departure; he keeps the effective, variable factors under systematic control, and watches the results. The psychiatric approach is the reversal of the experimental method. Our inquiry starts from the terminal point. We have to work our way backwards. We have to reconstruct the original conditions, as well as to determine the factors which, acting upon them, produced psychotic disturbances. There are two unknown quantities, which set a twofold task. Our problem demands, so to speak, two equations for its solution. The biography of a patient provides one of them only.

History determines the growth of a person; but the individual and his constitution predetermine his history. Individual history explains how a person actually became what he became; the species informs us what else he might have become. The thriving of a plant depends on soil, water, light, temperature. Yet, the same field on which one species grows in abundance furnishes a poor soil for another one. If we know the requirements of a species, then only are we able to state what historical conditions could have done and actually did to an individual specimen.

The discrimination of favorable from unfavorable environments refers to a standard which itself is not gained from history. It depends on a distinction between more and less perfect specimens. This distinction has the ideal type of the species for its third of comparison. The species is never completely realized in one individual, nor represented by an average of many of them. There is an approximation, only, to its ideal type. Closeness to or distance from it or pathological distortion tests the quality of individuals. In our evaluation of environmental conditions, we start from a concept of the species and an image of its ideal type. These enable us—as it were—to gauge the biographical factors, their range and limitations, and thereby to discriminate between the effects of "anlage" and environment, of pathological process and meaningful development. The sequence of natural events and the proceeding of our understanding are in a puzzling juxtaposition.

In this monograph the methodologically imposed order has been observed. The discussion of clinical problems follows the structural analysis of obsessions. In the first sections an attempt has been made to conceive the pathological structure of obsessive behavior, to demonstrate the concatenation of its manifold symptoms, to understand it as a functional unit and to relate the obsessive attitude to the peculiar world of the obsessive. In order to comprehend the specific morbidity of obsession we have had to contrast it with the norm. But there we have realized how deficient our knowledge of the norm is. Figure and ground have had to be worked out simultaneously. When we finally come to know the world in which the obsessive patient lives—not before this goal has been reached—, we may expect to understand its genesis. As we have intended to comprehend the obsessive world in its own right, we have shown due respect for the so-called surface phenomena. We have endeavoured to understand the manifest behavior of our patients without interpreting the conscious experience as only a representation of a more real, unconscious process. It seems in any case that, more often than not, the unconscious thoughts of patients are nothing but the conscious opinions of their physicians.

In a survey of a great number of case reports of obsessive patients one cannot help being impressed by the typical character of the disorder. Certainly there is no strict uniformity; in the clinical part of this paper several groups, differing in etiology, progress, and therapeutic responsiveness, have been discriminated. But no matter how much emphasis could be given to the individual drama, the homogeneity of cases belonging to one or the other of the various groups is striking.

The antagonism against the Kraepelinian era with its search for disease entities leads to the opposite extreme. I am afraid that, in overemphasizing the singularity of each case, we either utter a truism or commit a serious error. The medieval tenet "individuum est ineffabile" has lost none of its validity. If we had to work with completely unique cases, each one absolutely different from the other, we could not even describe them, much less comprehend or explain, teach or learn them. The particular is always a specification and limitation of the general. The understanding of an individual case therefore presupposes an understanding of the general and its variability. In our interpretation of a particular case we refer—whether we intend to or not—to a concept of the general. We cannot escape from this necessity. Even with all stress laid upon the particularities we have not freed ourselves from theoretical notions, but acquiesce in the admission of notions which grow more and more vague and confused.

In our medical activities we are confronted with an individual person who, for himself, uses the pronoun: "I." But everybody else does the same. I, the one who speaks, am an individual person, unique and irreplaceable, but at the same time I am anyone, one of many similar "I" 's. In the immediate contact of a conversation we realize who the one is who says "I" about himself, and addresses us as "you." But medical activity can never remain confined to the immediateness of the I-You relation. It does not suffice to know who the other one is; we want to know what he is. We think and speak together *about* our patients, signified by their proper names. The moment we examine or treat someone as a patient, we see him in a new relation, expressed by the third person of the pronoun, as "him" or "her," as a man, if not as "it," a body or organ, blood or heart, for example. As a patient the partner of our conversation becomes an object of our consideration and action.

In psychotherapy a certain ambiguity can hardly be avoided. The patient tries to enforce a personal I-You relation; the therapist yields to this tendency, but not without a mental reservation. As far as he plans and understands his own therapeutic actions he has to objectivate the personal relationships and has to transform the I-You into an I-He relation. While we speak with our patient, we actually speak to him. Being-opposite-to-each-other has taken the place of being-together. We may take a personal interest in our patient; we may become his friend; but, even so, as his physician we remain members of a profession, i.e., we act in a role which is general, using a knowledge which is general, and obeying rules which are general. The biographic-genetic method is not exempted. Conflict and solution, the genesis of conflicts and the goal of their solution, form the basic scheme of interpretation. Its uniform application to any case creates a paradoxical situation: apparently all attention is directed to the single case, but, in fact, the plenitude of phenomena is abandoned for the benefit of the scheme. In the search for a solution of the particular problems of individual obsessive patients we had found ourselves compelled to clarify our basic concepts, and to scrutinize the general presuppositions on which our interpretations and therapy rest.

I should like to acknowledge my indebtedness and express my gratitude to Dr. John C. Whitehorn, to whom I owe the opportunity to use the rich material of The Henry Phipps Psychiatric Clinic, The Johns Hopkins Hospital, and to write this monograph.

I am indebted to the California University Press, The Clarendon Press, Columbia University Press, Henry Holt and Co., Lea and Febiger, W. W. Norton and Co., and John Wiley and Sons for the permission to quote from several of their books.

I am deeply grateful to Drs. Hervey Cleckley, Kurt Goldstein, Walter Jahrreiss, Leo Kanner, Hans Loewald, and Esther Richards for their criticism and advice.

To Mrs. Anne Mangold I owe my sincere thanks for her helpful suggestions during the preparation of the manuscript.

ERWIN W. STRAUS

CONTENTS

ON OBSESSION

A CLINICAL AND METHODOLOGICAL STUDY

I

PROBLEMS OF METHOD

MUCH HAS BEEN SAID and much has been written about obsessions. Yet, obsessions still remain a tantalizing enigma both in theory and in practice. And it so happens that those who feel most secure on their theoretical grounds are most likely to be disappointed in practice. Binswanger has reported a conversation in which Freud once discussed this situation with him. I quote: "We discussed a severe case of obsessions in which we both had been interested for a long time. I wondered why such patients cannot take the last decisive step which the therapist expects them to take, why they cannot gain the ultimate psychoanalytical insight, and why, defying all preceding efforts, they remain in their misery. I assumed that there was no explanation for this failure of our patients other than a 'lack of spirituality,' an incapacity to elevate themselves to one plane of spiritual communication with their physician. On this level they would reach an understanding of certain 'unconscious drives.' A new view would open up to them. The self-denial enabling them to take the last decisive step would become possible." Freud agreed.[1]

In this conversation there is a sudden dramatic reversal in the therapeutic attitude. Critical examination yields to condemnation. The medical case has become a moral issue. The term "self-denial" refers to freedom in the ethical sense. The imputation is that the patient has been freed to act normally, but that he does not make the right use of his freedom.

The reference to freedom is no casual remark, which may slip into any conversation. In the "Ego and the Id" Freud speaks

[1] L. Binswanger: Freud und die Verfassung der Klinischen Psychiatrie, *Schweizer Archiv für Neurologie und Psychiatrie*, vol. 37, 1936, p. 177-199. In other works, preceding this paper, but following the conversation with Freud, which occurred in 1927, Binswanger emphasized the importance of considering pathological conditions as specific modes of human existence, completely detached from all negative biological evaluation and moralizing judgments. Cp. L. Binswanger: *Uber Ideenflucht*, Zurich 1933, p. 188.

about the efforts of psychoanalysis. It should not make, Freud says, pathological reactions impossible, but analysis should give to the Ego of the patient the *freedom* to decide for himself. One is justified in calling psychoanalysis a theory of human bondage and a technique for its alleviation.

I think Freud cannot be blamed for his reference to freedom. Psychiatry is always concerned with it. The question is whether or not we accept Freud's theory of freedom. However we decide, this decision will determine our views in any special psychiatric problem, especially when we discuss obsessions and compulsions.

NORM AND PATHOLOGY

Freud assumed, as we have seen, that in a certain phase of treatment the patient reaches the freedom to give up his obsessions, but refuses to do it. This sounds highly improbable. It seems to me that here Freud has become a captive of his own theory. A theory of bondage is not simply by implication also a theory of freedom. Freud, however, interpreted freedom as a minimum of bondage, applying the general psychoanalytical method of "hitting upon the norm by studying pathological conditions."[2] This method is closely connected—as will be seen later—with Freud's philosophical anthropology and cosmology. Only within that philosophy is the method justifiable. When we detach it from Freud's metapsychology and apply it as a universal method *per se*, we are losing ground.

In psychopathology the situation is no other than that in pathology in general. As long as we do not know the structure of the norm we are unable to recognize that which, undergoing a change in a pathological process, emerges in a distorted shape. Consequently, the structure of the pathological state itself is incomprehensible and the pathogenesis remains uncertain. Without Harvey's work, clinicians could never have ordered the scattered symptomatology of the disturbances of circulation into a meaningful whole. In order to understand a change we have to know both the final stage and the initial one. Conjectures are unavoidable where there is no direct access to the object of our

[2]S. Freud: Die Disposition zur Zwangsneurose. Ein Beitrag zum Problem der Neurosenwahl (1913), reprinted in *Schriften zur Neurosenlehre*, Intern. psa. Verlag, Vienna, 1931.

curiosity. But where the way for inquiry is open, we should use it. Therefore, my attention will be given first to the norm, which we find disturbed in a peculiar way in cases of obsessions. This involves another deviation from familiar methods.

BIOGRAPHY AND STRUCTURAL ANALYSIS

With Darwin and Freud many have come to believe that we have understood something if we know how it came to pass. Consequently, the right method will be genetic. Even if the assumption were correct, the procedure of historical reconstruction remains a very deceptive technique. Let me give an example: an obsessive patient, Annette M., blames her mother for all her troubles. "Mother was sapping my strength as a vacuum cleaner takes up dust." Her sister, however, describes the situation as follows: "The feeling that she should take care of mother is quite preposterous. Mother has always been a strong, healthy woman, perfectly capable of taking care of herself. . . . She has always given Annette everything in her power, even when it meant sacrifices to the point of hardship. . . . I have never known Annette to give up anything for mother. . . . She has tyrannized over mother in every way. . . ." In the reconstruction of a life history we start from statements which are never simple descriptions of facts. They are personal reactions and interpretations of conditions which frequently the reporters themselves have helped to produce. Biographers could be satisfied to find out how a person sees his own past. Physicians cannot stop there. Therapy always presupposes the existence of potentialities not realized in a case history. Therefore, we have to know not only how things actually came about, but how they might have turned out otherwise. We could evaluate better the meaning and importance of biographical events if we knew more about the initial conditions. As the "anlagen" are neither infinite in their plasticity nor equal in their limitations, we cannot disregard them. Unfortunately, we have in an individual case no direct knowledge about the original constitution, its plasticity and limitation. In our reconstruction of the past we have events, little known in their significance, working on a completely unknown substance.

This is certainly a method with a very broad margin of error.

The genetic method could well stand a supplementation by other methods, which would permit us to reduce this margin.

Actually, we make constant use of a comparative method; we could not take one step without it. When we accept someone as a patient, say an obsessive, we do it because we take him to be a pathological case, because we recognize a deviation from the norm. We use a comparative method, but in a most imperfect way. The norm is familiar to us; in acting it out, we find someone who does not cooperate with us, who behaves in a "strange" way. The norm then is familiar to us, yet it is unknown. So far we are in no way ahead of the average layman, who also acts normally without understanding the norm. In everyday life we do not need such knowledge; in psychiatry we do; and, as psychology fails to give us an understanding of the norm, we have to do this job ourselves.

THE IMPORTANCE OF THE "SURFACE PHENOMENA"

The genetic method does not strengthen respect for conscious experience. It is evaluated, or better it is devaluated, as a mere superstructure. Like divining-rod-walkers, who direct their interest to the treasures hidden beneath the surface, many psychotherapists turn their attention almost exclusively to the unconscious and to the past, thereby neglecting the analysis of the "surface" phenomena.

As a consequence, the term "obsessive" is frequently used in a somewhat indiscriminate way. A marked inclination towards order, neatness, perfection, may be labeled as obsessive,—a clear example of interpreting the norm from pathological states. In turn, factors which may contribute to the acquisition of orderliness and cleanliness are used for an understanding of pathological cases. I am afraid that in mixing phenomena which do not belong together we will fail to see the very morbidity of obsessions. Even if we restrict the term "obsessive" to undoubtedly pathological cases, we probably still comprise under one heading widely different groups. From personal experience and from the study of a number of older case records at The Henry Phipps Clinic I have become convinced—as others have before me—that we should divide obsessives into several subgroups.

The genesis, the development, the symptomatology, the outcome, the behavior in the ward, the relation to the clinic, are typical for each group. A distinction of these groups has also a practical value for prognosis and therapy.

The subgroup in which I am most interested is well characterized in a letter written by an obsessive patient. I quote some sentences from this letter:

"In November 1918, a flower bouquet was placed on my bed. My cousin, who had a charming little boy two years old, took the bouquet from the bed, saying, 'It is not right to put flowers on a bed.' Three weeks later the child was . From this time on I was very careful never to put flowers on the bed. I am very fond of beautiful flowers, but I cannot touch them any more, and I cannot stand having them in my apartment. But this happened only after I had had a child of my own, who was one and a half years old at that time. I was constantly afraid that the child might be taken from me. In January 1931, a very dear, good old friend, who belonged one could say to our family . His wife, who had hardly any friends and relatives, was with us nearly every Sunday after she had visited the That wasn't troubling to me in the beginning. Yet, after approximately four to six months I became alarmed by her gloves, later on also by her coat and her shoes. I was careful that none of these things ever came too near to ours. That went on in this way for a while until the woman noticed it and did not come any more because she felt I was disgusted. As we live near to the , I am getting excited about all these people going there. It is a real pilgrimage. If one of these persons touches me I have to clean or wash the particular piece of cloth, either with soap or benzine. If it happens that some of these people enter our home, I cannot move any more. I feel as if the room would get quite narrow and that I could not avoid touching all the things with my dress. I have to go through the door edgeways. To find peace again I have to wash everything with soap and water. Then everything becomes large and wide, and I can move again. If I do some errands and there is somebody in the store, I cannot go in because they may touch me, or I may get the money which was theirs before. So I am restless all day long, and the restlessness never leaves me. Either I have to wipe things off, or dust, or wash. As soon as I sit down for a while I feel so tired that I fall asleep wherever I am. Nowhere can I find repose. If I ride on the streetcar, I am always worried for fear that somebody may step in, wearing . If that should happen and the woman or the man should take a seat near to me, I should have to get off. Also pictures in newspapers or magazines, where such things are shown, disturb me greatly. If my hand touches such a printed spot, I have to wash it thoroughly again. I cannot find words enough for all the things which hound me. Inwardly I am constantly in an uproar and for me the saying is true, "There, where you are not, there is rest."

II

DISGUST A CENTRAL THEME OF OBSESSIONS

THE LETTER just quoted indicates the theme of many obsessions: death and decay.[1] The omission of these very words reveals a fear of some magic power. In writing, things, signified by the omitted words, gain for the patient immediate sensory reality. Likewise, the patient avoids tactile contact with obituaries or the announcements of death in a newspaper. She is obviously afraid of contamination because the printed signs, symbolizing death, have become infested with the sensory presence of death itself. The hostile power first spotted at one place expands, and this process of diffusion seems to have no limits whatsoever. Death, as the letter of the patient expresses, is ubiquitous, amorphous, ungraspable. It exists as an infinite potentiality, as a demonic power, which scoffs at all counteraction. Yet the patient cannot stop fighting it. But in all this activity there is no real action that leads from a start to a goal. There is no real, definite object for action either. The germs which so many patients fight are objects, but as invisible and ungraspable objects the germs are the most perfect expression of the omnipresence and the omnipotence of the dreadful, from which there is no escape. Day after day is consumed in a desperate and futile struggle. There is no more progress in the lives of the patients. Their history comes to a standstill and also the space in which the patients can move freely shrinks. They are confined to a street, to a house, to a room, to a corner of a room. Our patient describes this narrowing of space as a direct sensory experience. Space has no rigid shape; it unfolds, widens and narrows, in accordance with the dynamics of the I-world relations.

Obsessive patients live in a strange world, basically different from the world familiar to us. If we want to understand children, we have to understand them in their own world. If we want to understand obsessives, we have to understand them in the world

[1]Cp. E. Straus: Ein Beitrag zur Pathologie der Zwangserscheinungen, *Monatsschrift fuer Psychiatrie und Neurologie,* vol. 98, 1938, p. 61-101.

peculiar to them. Study of behavior always requires a knowledge of the specific structure of the world in which a species, man or animal, groups or individuals, behave. The world in which the obsessives live has such a structure that their behavior is dominated by horror and dread, not because of fear of death which may hit them in the near future, but because of the presence of death in sensory immediateness, warded off in disgust. Thus we are led to the phenomenon of disgust and an analysis of its structure and norm.

PSYCHOLOGY AND PSYCHOPATHOLOGY OF DISGUST

The importance of disgust and its opposite is obvious. There is practically no moment in our everyday life into which disgust or delight do not enter.

Unfortunately psychology has not much to say about disgust. Starting, then, from scratch, we may first look for objects which usually arouse disgust. And it seems that there are some that cause disgust as regularly as light produces a pupillary contraction. Disgust then could be a response to typical stimuli, and we might even think of determining their chemical structure. Consequently, we should have to interpret disgust and its pathology in line with the James-Lange theory of emotion. James gave to his theory the paradoxical formulation: we do not cry, strike, or tremble, because we are sorry, angry, or fearful, but we are sorry because we cry, angry because we strike, fearful because we tremble.[2] Using this formula we could say we do not vomit because we have come in contact with something disgusting, but we feel disgusted because we are nauseated. But even those who do not refuse James' theory of emotions would hesitate to apply it to disgust.

While there are a few objects which produce disgust in the majority of cases, there are many others which are disgusting for one group but indifferent or even attractive for another. Many of us abhor horse meat; pork is disgusting to an orthodox Jew; the Russian peasants are bewildered that we can eat such

[2]W. James: *Principles of Psychology,* New York, Henry Holt and Co., reprinted 1923, Vol. II, p. 450. By permission of Henry Holt and Co., Inc. Copyright, 1890 by Henry Holt and Company. Copyright, 1918 by Alice H. James.

disgusting things as Camembert cheese. And do not children at a certain age play with dirt, showing no signs of disgust at all?

Considering all these variations, a conclusion strictly opposed to the first one is—as it seems—unavoidable. Disgust, far from being an unconditional physiological response, is a psychological reaction acquired under the influence of certain social conventions. In disgust we react to taboos set up by society. There we have the old distinction of natural and conventional. Society forbids actions to which by nature we have definite propensities. It is clear how this rash assumption, as an interpretation of the norm, also leads to certain interpretations in pathology. In every interpretation of pathological cases an interpretation of the norm is openly or silently anticipated.

If the variability of objects of disgust cannot be denied, is the convention hypothesis therefore justified? Through customs and habits many things acquire a disgusting character. However, conventions do not work as well in the opposite direction. They cannot remove disgusting characteristics. As doctors we learn to deal with urine and sweat and what not. But outside of the laboratory the original character persists. We can deal with those things because we are able to change our attitude, i.e., our mode of contact. Through our attitudes objects gain a certain physiognomy, to which we react.

In the norm the plasticity of objects is not infinite; our attitudes towards them, in disgust as in other cases, show a definite structure. While the choice of objects is dependent on conventions, the basic attitude is no product of social conditions. To give another example: whether we learn to speak English, French, or German, as our mother tongue,—that depends on our environment and its conventions. Nevertheless, Language with a capital L and our capacity to speak are a part of human nature.

The Proteus-like character of disgusting material seems to frustrate every effort to determine in general the physiognomy to which we react in disgust. Yet, in the sudden changes of a single case, where variability reaches its height, the basic attitude of disgust becomes understandable. Objects of disgust not only vary from one case to the other; they even vary with the same person. The smell of a steak which was so attractive while we were hungry becomes repulsive when we return into the dining room after the meal. Certainly society has not taught this change of attitude, which is pretty much the same for all of us. Steak before dinner and steak after dinner—I do not speak of the one which has been eaten already—have the same chemical and physical qualities. But they are different in their sensual appeal. In sensory experience all things are *objects for me.* As thinking beings, or as observers in everyday life, and still more as scientific observers, we divorce things from this original sensory relation; we determine things and their qualities in an impersonal, general, unchanging, frame of reference. There they are the same at all times and for everybody. Mathematical physics is the classic example. In measuring I compare one length with another length; I abstract completely from any relation things have to me. Disgust and delight we experience not as neutral observers, but as individual, living beings. As living beings we experience the world in relation to us, to our individual, vital, existences, i.e., in unifying and separating. In sensory experience we always experience the world *and* ourselves in different modes of contact and direction, and in varying degrees of distance and closeness.

The modes of contact vary with every sense. I may see some dirt on the street and pass it with indifference, but I should feel disgusted in touching it with my bare foot, and still more with my hand or my mouth. In each instance there is a different distance and, therefore, a different meaning of unification, which I vehemently resist in the case of disgusting things. My capacity for and inclination toward unification and separation will lend to things the physiognomy of delight or disgust; on the other hand, it is the delightful or disgusting physiognomy of things which will stimulate my inclination toward or away from unification.

Physiognomical qualities cannot be measured; they cannot be localized. We can measure distances, but not width or narrowness of space. In measuring we break a distance into parts. But width or narrowness are qualities which belong to the totality of visible space. They cannot be broken into parts. A long distance is a multiple of a small one. A wide space is not the multiple of a narrow one. Width is not here or there; it cannot be located or demarcated in its physiognomical qualities. Physiognomical qualities float through space; they emanate; they also take possession of us; we are widened and narrowed down with the width or narrowness of space. But as our patient said in her letter, space widens and shrinks according to our own vital moods. Physiognomical qualities, because they are not measurable, resist the attack of natural science, which therefore neglects them, while in the practice of our everyday life and in the magic interpretation of the world they are of first importance.

THE PHYSIOGNOMY OF DECAY

Although disgust, like the other physiognomical characters, is not a quality which can be measured, located or objectively identified, it is no mere X which evades all determination. Here again the variability may enable us to find the permanent character.

Curls on a head look lovely and attractive, but the same hair found in the soup is disgusting; perhaps we should like to cut one of these curls as a souvenir, but we should be disgusted to collect the hair left in a comb. Saliva spit out is disgusting, an expression of our contempt, but on fresh lips and tongue the saliva is not disgusting. Separation from the integrity of the living organism turns the physiognomy from delight to disgust. This separation indicates a transition from life to death; it signifies decay. Disgust is directed more against decay, the process of decomposition, than against the dead. A skeleton, a mummy, may be frightening, even horrible, but not as disgusting as a cadaver which has just been brought from a river to the morgue.

A catalog of things repudiated by disgust could never be complete. In spite of the great variability of disgusting objects, the reaction of disgust is not the result of arbitrary and artificial interdictions; disgust is a natural reaction; it obeys a physiognomic law. Manifold factors cooperate in the shaping of physiognomies; custom is but one factor among many.

Since the context in which something presents itself frequently decides whether we will be attracted by it or frightened away, whether we will see in it the physiognomy of decay or of life, the same matter can express abundance, the growing life, or decomposition, the passing away. The sweat of an athlete who has just won the contest will not prevent his girl friend from embracing him. The perspiration which covers the face of the sick has quite another effect. The difference is determined by the difference of context to which the parts belong. In the first case, sweat, breathlessness, even exhaustion, still carry the expression of strong, healthy life. They express the lavishness of someone who can afford it. Although in the second case a loving soul may overcome all initial sensual aversions, yet in kissing the sick one, as St. Francis kissed the leper, one does not follow a longing for unification. The legend reports that St. Francis first passed the leper. When he had turned his horse back and had approached the outcast, he found the strength to express a charity which reaches beyond disgust, sickness, and death. In hearing this story, we of today at once have a suspicion of neurotic tendencies. It may be well, therefore, to remember that the doctor of old had to taste urine (hence the term *diabetes mellitus*). Laboratory techniques have freed us from this painful duty, but others remain. Every doctor, and still more every nurse, is expected to serve a patient with actions not less disgusting. The question what power enables us to overcome primary sensory tendencies while they continue to work is still unanswered.

The physiognomical ambiguity of disgusting matters has a deep reason. In our talk and our thoughts we oppose life to death, and in opposing one to the other, we separate them, as if they were two different entities. In the living organism, however, life and death are closely interwoven. The skin, in growing, in rejuvenating itself, produces its own waste. So do all other organs. The more vigorous the vital processes, the more luxuriant the bodily functions, the greater the waste.

The biological terms, metabolism, assimilation or dissimilation, aim at these phenomena. But the biological terminology is not appropriate here. A stanza of poetry would do better than a scientific formula. In scientific notions, in abstract formulas, the original physiognomic meaning vanishes. Only a few understand scientific language, and these few have to be taught this idiom for many years. The language of senses is understandable for everybody, everywhere, at all times, without instruction. The reason is clear. In the laboratory, in the library, at his desk, the scientist meditates about things; he wants to establish a relation between the process x and the process y, not between these processes and himself. The observer is not interposed as "this single individual" in the processes which he observes. Disgust and delight, attraction and repulsion, I, as this single individual, experience at this concrete moment, here and now. There is a relation between me and the object of disgust. It is directed towards me and I towards it. In this case I am no longer an observer who keeps himself at a distance. I am in the game myself, in my potentialities of uniting and separating.

SYMPATHETIC RELATIONS TO THE WORLD AND THEIR VARIETIES

Since life and death, blooming and fading, dwell so closely together in the living organism, and since physiognomies make their appearance only within the direct sensory I-world relation, it will depend also on us whether we will find the physiognomy of living or of dying. It will depend on our inclination and capacity to unite. For the friends of Rubens the world bears a different impress than for the followers of Malthus. Franz Hals painted ragamuffins and hoboes who, in their tatters, look richer than many of Van Dyck's princes in si k and brocade. Dutch still-lifes of the seventeenth century assure us that nature has set the table plentifully. Painters of a later epoch, in the midst of commodities undreamed of by their predecessors, discovered nothing but scarcity, want, indigence. "Still-life" says the English language, "nature morte" the French. Sometimes indeed our grip is more important than the matter we lay hand upon. Hunger is the best cook.

For a young, healthy boy the plate cannot be full enough. But what dietitian does not know that to put a full plate in front of a sick person is a certain means of frightening away his weak appetite? One has to be equal to abundance.

"If appetite and hunger are lacking, apathy instead of interest characterizes our attitude towards the viands of the table. In those circumstances, even if food is chewed and swallowed, the absence of enjoyment is not propitious for a tonic state of the gastro-intestinal muscle and for a rich secretion of the digestive fluids. . . . On the other hand, a hearty appetite, gusto and pleasure in eating, are highly advantageous conditions. They are typical of abundant bodily vigor and they contribute to perpetuation of that vigor. Just as there may be a vicious circle of weakness, indifference to the pleasures of the palate, a trifling acceptance of nourishment, and a consequently continued weakness, so, contrariwise, there may be a beneficial circle of energetic activity, eager enjoyment of food, and a sufficient food supply, well digested, to sustain a further display of energy."[3]

The sick and the weak man is frightened by abundance. He retreats from the world and withdraws into himself. The healthy and the strong man is attracted by exuberance. He discovers the physiognomy of abundance. He enjoys his growth; he reaches beyond himself to conquer the world or to give himself up to it.

"Oh, Edward!" complains Coleridge,[4] "we receive but what we give,
And in our life alone does nature live.
Ours is her wedding-garment, ours her shroud! . . .
Ah! from the soul itself must issue forth
A light, a glory, a fair luminous cloud enveloping the earth—
And from the soul must there be sent
A sweet and potent voice, of its own birth,
Of all sweet sounds the life and element."

To the eye, turned back on retreat from beauty, the view is changed. On a bright day, life is still more a burden to the depressive. Abundance is not seen any longer as ab-undant, i.e., as the fecund wave flowing over the too narrow borders. Abundance, as Rubens painted it, is seen as a shapeless mass, exuberance as obesity, procreation as pollution. In retreat from abundance the autumnal beauty may come in sight, fall in its sweet melancholy. We feel attracted by waning life, but still by life. One step downward and the emphasis is shifted from life in

[3]Walter B. Cannon: *Digestion and Health,* New York, Norton and Co., 1936, p. 118. Reprinted by permission of the publishers, W. W. Norton & Company, Inc., New York. Copyright 1936 by the publishers.

[4]S. Coleridge: *Dejection. An Ode.*

decline to the decline of life: the theme and tune of Baudelaire's work and existence.[5]

And there are others who, not being equal to abundance, turn against it. Thus, Swift's Gulliver tells of his voyage to Brobdingnag: "The nurse of the giant baby was forced to supply the last remedy by giving it suck. I must confess no object ever disgusted me so much as the sight of her monstrous breast. . . . It stood prominent six foot, and could not be less than sixteen in circumference. The nipple was about half the bigness of my head, and the hue both of that and the dug so varified with spots, pimples, and freckles that nothing could appear more nauseous; for I had a near sight of her, she sitting down the more conveniently to give suck, and I standing on the table. This made me reflect upon the fair skins of our English ladies, who appear so beautiful to us, only because they are of our own size, and their defects not to be seen but through a magnifying glass, where we find by experiment that the smoothest and whitest skins look rough and coarse, and ill coloured." The effects of the magnifying glass are one of Swift's favorite themes. In using the glass he ever has proved a master. Through grotesque enlargements, through fetishistic dismemberment, he shows the mud and slime, the germs, which pervade everything. We know from Swift's biographers his kinship to the obsessive, and we also know how much this obsessive character influenced his political and literary activities.

Sensitized by resentment and envy some espy the flaws and deficiencies in everything; they are happy enough to uncover them: that "the poor world is pestered with such waterflies, diminutives of nature" is no frightening discovery for Shakespeare's Thersites. Wherever he looks he finds "nothing but lechery, all incontinent varlets." If there is a spare moment when he cannot see around him patchery and juggling, he invents new evils of his own imagination. When he enters the stage for the first time he thinks aloud: "Agamemnon—how,

[5]In his "Journal Intime" Baudelaire wrote: "Since my childhood the sense of solitude. In spite of my family, above all when surrounded by my comrades the sense of a destiny eternally solitary. Yet a taste for life and for pleasure which is very keen." On another day he wrote: "Woman is natural, that is to say abominable."

if he had boils? Full, all over, generally? And those boils did run? —Say so,—did not the general run then? were not that a botchy core?—Then would come some matter from him; I see none now." Thersites is a bastard,—he says it; he is a coward,—he knows it. It gives him the freedom to despise and to revile. His vocabulary of invectives and filth is unlimited. His wishes for Patroclus are the "rotten diseases of the south, the guts-griping, ruptures, catarrhs, loads o'gravel i' the back, lethargies, cold palsies, raw eyes, dirt-rotten livers, wheezing lungs, bladders full of imposthume, sciaticas, limekilns i' the palm, incurable bone-ache, and the rivelled fee-simple of the tetter." He implores "the vengeance on the whole camp! or rather the Neapolitan bone-ache!" and ends his curse: "I have said my prayers, and devil, envy, say Amen."[6]

When finally the power to revile fails, the beaten persecutor becomes himself persecuted: the Neapolitan bone-ache, the rotten diseases of the south, the guts griping, ruptures, catarrhs, the wheezing lungs, the dirt-rotten livers, the bladders full of imposthume, are all coming after him. He is frightened by the mere names, for which Thersites has an insatiable desire. In this world of sickness and putrefaction, the obsessives live. It is a world like that shown in the paintings of Hieronymus Bosch.

OBSESSION, A DISTURBANCE OF THE SYMPATHETIC RELATIONS TO THE WORLD

Obsessions belong to the pathology of the sympathetic relations which connect man with his world. There is a disturbance in the balance between making and marring, between the awareness of abundance and that of decay. The view of obsessives is confined to the aspect of the loathsome. Their existence has been shifted to the one pole of the polaric unity. They are no longer able to discover anything but the physiognomy of decay. But it should be borne in mind that we are not passive in the sight of physiognomies, but that we cooperate in shaping them.

[6] I have quoted Thersites as if he were a patient of mine. Indeed, in the "dramatis personae" a great poet creates characters which are purer and clearer cases than those we meet on our wards. The relationship is comparable to the one between laws, formulated in the equations of physics, and empirical observations. The laws refer to ideal structures, never perfectly realized in a concrete case.

Annette M. could not understand why children grow up. The case history adds: "She means this in a bodily sense." She was frightened—as we shall see later—by the physiognomy of death, of decline, of time ticking away. She was not interested in the histology or physiology of growth. She was puzzled that there was growth. Her amazement expressed her own incapacity to realize in emotional sympathy that there was growth, life in expansion.

The disturbance of the balance of sympathetic relations has these consequences:

1. The physiognomic becomes predominant; all other relations to the world are overpowered by this one.

2. The physiognomy which emerges is always that of deformation.[7] It appears as decay, disease, dirt, as death, corpse, decomposition, as germs, dust, mud, as excretion, urine, faeces, as sweat, sperma, sputum,—a thousand shapes of the destructive, the negative, the evil.

3. The world grows homogeneous because of the omnipresence of decay. As there are no forces to counterbalance its exclusive sway, no zone of indifference enables the obsessives to have at its extreme ends individual things acting as the exclusive carriers either of abundance or of decay. Normally we can surround ourselves with attractive things and expel the others to a sequestered spot.

4. The world of the obsessive has lost such a polaric articulation. One interconnection only is left: that between the evils which intrude from all sides and the asylum which the obsessive tries to defend. In his obsessive actions he tries to protect his last redoubt against calamitous invasion.

TWO GENERAL PRESUPPOSITIONS OF THIS VIEW

All that has been said about disgust and obsessions is based on certain general assumptions. This is a matter of course, not worth mentioning, were it not for the fact that these assumptions contradict other principles, time-honored, and, therefore, more by habit than insight, frequently taken for granted. One of them

[7]E. V. v Gebsattel in his study: Die Welt der Zwangskranken, *Monatsschrift für Psychiatrie und Neurologie*, vol. 99, 1938, p. 10-74, speaks about an Anti-eidos.

is the tenet that all psychological experience, since it only accompanies physiological processes, has to be reduced to the underlying physiological events, assimilated to their structure, and explained in accordance with the methods of natural science. "To understand man, the doer, we must understand his nervous system, for upon it his actions depend."[8] Another principle, somewhat younger in date, can be briefly expressed by the single term: pleasure-principle. This is not the place for a thorough discussion of general doctrines. In defense, only, of my own view I cannot dispense with a short discussion of my dissension.

1) In my analysis of disgust I have not referred to the stimulus-response scheme. I could not make use of it because the experience of disgust does not fit into this pattern. I wonder whether there is any psychological experience that could be described—to say nothing of understood—in strict analogy with physiological processes.

For sensory experience there are no stimuli, but rather objects. In sensory experience we are directed to objects as to The Other. This character of sensory experience is irreducible. The peculiar relation through which we, here, are connected with the objects of our sensory experience, over there, belies the geometrical pattern of space with its order of side by side. In perceiving we reach beyond the limits of our bodies. By one and the same act we experience ourselves *and* the world. We could as well say the world *and* ourselves.

Physiology necessarily breaks this polaric unity into two different events, one occurring outside of the body (the stimulus), the other one inside (the response). The sense-organs are interpreted as receivers. What do they receive? Energies of physical agents in the environment of a human body. By the interference of such external agents another process within the body is initiated. This second process, once set in motion, is completely detached from the "outside." Physiological methods isolate an organism within its environment from its environment; psychological experience connects man with his world. Sensory experience, although dependent, is in its content not congruous,

[8]E. Boring, H. Langfeld, H. Weld: *Introduction to Psychology*, John Wiley & Sons, New York, 1939, p. 3. Reprinted by permission of John Wiley & Sons, Inc.

parallel, isomorphous, to the physiological processes. Experience does not begin within a solitary organism which is aware of itself, of its "sensations," before it is aware of the world. It is the basic phenomenon of sensory experience that we are—at the same time—aware of the world and of ourselves; not the one alone; not the one earlier than the other.

2) Freud—at least in his theory—did not deviate from traditional biologism. Drives belong to an isolated organism. The drives are blind; they have no primary relation to the world. They originate and they reach their goal within the boundaries of an organism. Freud emphasized most strongly the unimportance of the object. ". . . this flexible libido works in the service of the pleasure-principle in order to avoid a damming up of energy and to facilitate its discharge. There is, no doubt, a certain indifference as to how the discharge occurs, provided it does occur. We are familiar with this trait as characteristic of cathectic processes in the Id. It is found in erotic cathexes, where the indifference toward the object is marked; it becomes especially noticeable in analytic transferences, which occur regardless of the individuality of the therapist. Rank recently offered good examples of the fact that neurotic revenge may be directed against others than the proper persons. Such behavior of the unconscious makes one think of a story told humorously: one of the three village tailors to be hanged because the only village blacksmith had committed a mortal crime. Punishment simply has to be meted out, even if it does not fall upon the culprit."[9]

Libido may be fixed on other persons (Objekt-besetzung). The other person then becomes an object for the drive. The true goal of the libidinous drive, however, remains always the same: to gain pleasure. This satisfaction is obtained in a certain physical state by the reduction of tension. Freud assumes "that pain corresponds to an increase, pleasure to a decrease, of this quantity of stimulation present in physical life."[10] Stimuli are disturbances, whether they have their origin inside or outside of the body.

[9]S. Freud: *Das Ich und das Es*, Intern. psa. Verlag, Vienna, 1923, p. 55 f.
[10]S. Freud: *Jenseits des Lustprinzips*, Vienna, 1921, p. 4.

Pleasure is experienced in withdrawing from the world, by turning inward into ourselves, and finally by sleep. Freud has left no doubt that both drives, Eros and Death-instinct, aim at the same goals: sleep and death. "Based upon theoretical considerations supported by biology, we assumed the existence of a Death instinct, its task being to reduce organic life to an inanimate state. Eros, in contrast, aims at the goal of organizing life through an ever increasing integration of living matter heretofore shattered into particles. Thereby, of course, Eros aims to preserve life. Both drives are almost reactionary in their striving towards the restoration of conditions thrown into unbalance by the genesis of life. If so, the genesis of life would simultaneously be the cause of both, of its preservation and of the urge towards death. Life itself is a struggle and compromise between these two aims."[11] Life is a disturbance of the inanimate. Both the instincts, Eros and Death-instinct, endeavour to reestablish the order disturbed by the emergence of life. We do not enjoy the world as the scene of our self-realization.

The metapsychological writings belong to the late period of Freud's work. His philosophy of nature is, nevertheless, the basis of his philosophical anthropology, i.e., of his interpretation of the human world and of human existence.[12]

Freud was not afraid of using mythological terms; Eros and Death-instinct are cosmic forces. It is a sign of Freud's greatness that he could write a modern myth in books which have the paraphernalia of scientific writings. Perhaps this was the only way to make a myth palatable to modern men. They are willing to accept it, provided it is empirical and scientifically demonstrated. Freud knew better; he coined the term "metapsychology," and at least once in the "Psychology of Masses" he called his own hypothesis a myth. But sometimes he, too, confused his cosmological visions with terrestrial experience.

In blending traditional biologism with his cosmology, Freud

[11]S. Freud: *Das Ich und das Es.* Internat. psa. Verlag, Vienna, 1923, p. 49.

[12]L. Binswanger has discussed this problem intensively. Besides the paper already mentioned, compare "La Conception de l'homme chez Freud à la lumière de L'Anthropologie Philosophique," *L'Evolution Psychiatrique*, vol. I, 1938, pp. 3-35. See also Binswanger's clinical study: "Der Fall Ellen West," *Schweizer Archiv für Psychiatrie und Neurologie*, vols. 53 (1943); 54 (1944); 55 (1945).

added a new and most characteristic note. The organism is shaped by Eros and Death-instinct. As experience only *represents* these unconscious cosmic forces, the ultimate meaning of all our needs and desires reflects the tendencies of those forces to turn life back to death, to inanimate matter. Life is a macabre dance towards death. We, the dancers, are poor, cheated fools. In this somber pessimism the pathological and the norm lose all distinctive meaning. We want to gain pleasure; but in striving for it we are busy eliminating stimulation, discharging energy, turning away from the world, going back to sleep. Therefore seeing and hearing play such a negligible role in psychoanalysis. Man is viewed within the horizon of his lower senses. Among all senses seeing is the one to which the hypotheses of the pleasure-principle are least applicable. In seeing, our interest is with the objects and our enjoyment also.

This being-related-to-the-world becomes noticeable at a very early stage in childhood. "She nursed from the first with energy, and with an expression of great content . . . ," writes Millicent Shinn about her niece, "still, from the first, there was just as marked an appearance of pleasure in the bath, and after the middle of the second month, demonstrations of much higher pleasure in sights, such as faces, a spot of sunlight, stripes of color."[13] Comparing the desire for food with other interests Miss Shinn says: ". . . with these exceptions food is always mentioned in a subordinate place among the regular objects of desire, after such things as pictures, learning words, exploring mysteries, jouncing on mattress springs, dolls, playing with books, etc. She was almost always ready, after satisfying the first hunger, to desert the breast for a frolic, to listen, look about, and play." All observers of healthy children have found in them the same kind of enjoyment. The world is not received as a disturbance, as a group of stimuli, causing an unpleasant increase of tension; there is a "craving for the stimulus, a tension and discomfort in its absence." Among the pleasures that gave livelier joy than food, Miss Shinn reports, from the thirteenth month, such things as "going out to see the moon, which caused a passion of joy." The

[13] M. W. Shinn: *Notes on the Development of a Child.* Berkeley, The University Press, 1893-1899, repr. 1909, vol. I, p. 216 ff.

view of the moon, the seeing of things, fulfills, then, a basic need. The discovery of the world is not directed by fear only, or by the intention to swallow things to incorporate them into the body; there is something at work, astonishment, wonder, an intellectual curiosity, which soon will reach its final form: breaking through the sensory horizon.

Light opens the world to us. Light is, in physiological terms, a stimulus. With dawn we experience an increase of stimuli. But who has never seen with the greatest joy the awakening of a day? In seeing we are turned towards the world, and in seeing it we find pleasure. The eyes are as insatiable as they are indefatigable. We climb a mountain or a tower to enjoy the view. We are not afraid of an increase of stimuli. We are ready for it, i.e., ready to enjoy seeing the visible world in the width of an open horizon. In fatigue we welcome darkness; in sickness we close our eyes; then the world has become a burden for us. As long as we are not yet overwhelmed by fatigue, sickness, or old age, the world is the stage of our self-realization, not only of the maintenance of our lives, but of our growth and expansion. We are not content with mere preservation.

For the physiologist the senses are receivers; for the psychologist they are mediators between man and the world. Only in relation to the world do we experience ourselves. Our satisfaction and dissatisfaction is embedded in this relationship. Whether we succeed or fail in our unification with the world determines our enjoyment or our distress.

Objects are exchangeable; *the* object is not. It cannot be absent. A boy who grew up in Baltimore will fall in love, say, with Betty; in Savannah it would be Mary, and Ruth in Denver. At each place he would have found a girl, i.e., another human being, a You, a woman, a young one, a pretty one. Generic qualities determine meaning and value of individual objects. They determine the character of the subject also; for our boy acts in his choice, likewise, as a human being, a man, a young one, etc. He will grow an individuality the more he finds the generic qualities incorporated in that one individual who, thereby, becomes *the* one. In relation to the irreplacable one, we first find our deepest joy and pleasure.

The village tailor may be hanged instead of the village blacksmith. However, a rat, a tree, a chair would not do the job, not even in a comic story. Objects are exchangeable as far as they participate in the same generic qualities. A girl cannot be replaced by a dog, a mare, a hen. Among our patients we will meet one who used such strange substitutes. But he was an obsessive; he lived in a basically distorted world. Whatever we are we are only in a specific relation to an object, as a part and member of an I-world relationship.

The pleasure-principle ascribes to sleep supremacy over awakeness; sleep is the goal, awakeness a disturbance, caused by reality. This theory interchanges norm and pathological states. If we accept its tenets, we cannot understand the joyful abundance which Cannon described, or the physiognomic vitalization which Coleridge praises. Consequently, we are prevented from understanding the physiognomic morbidity which occurs in obsessions.

Here we may well dismiss the general presuppositions and return to the discussion of obsessions.

III

THE WORLD OF OBSESSIVES AND THE SYMPTOMATOLOGY OF OBSESSIONS

THE OBSESSIVE LIVES and experiences in a world deranged in its basic structure. This peculiar and strange world is the scene of his actions, his orderliness, his stinginess, his rituals. Once set, the stage no longer leaves to the actor any choice of the role he wants to play. The social behavior of the obsessive is predetermined by the structural change in the physiognomy of the world. Our next task, then, is to turn to the details and to demonstrate how the symptomatology of obsessions is moulded in all its aspects by the disturbance of the sympathetic relations.

ACTION AND PERFECTIONISM

In the routine of everyday life the obsessive finds his way blocked by obstacles which do not impede the course of a healthy person. Actions as simple as locking a door or turning off the gas switch swell to gigantic tasks. The writing of a necessary letter is a catastrophic event, even if the letter is to contain no more than a few polite or neutral sentences. Days will be spent in preparation, in phrasing and rephrasing the draft. After the letter is finally written, new exertions will be necessary when it comes to addressing and sealing it. Yet the greatest difficulty is still impending: the mailing. But the mailing does not terminate the issue; it marks the beginning of a new phase of doubts and scruples.

In such trifling matters, which do not yet belong to the proper ritual, the obsessive cannot come to an end, but to no real start either. Every step is threatened by hesitation and indecision, by the need to recapitulate and control and annul. Even if all has been done, nothing has been accomplished.

The obsessives find themselves in such a predicament apparently because the execution of their action depends on expectations unrealizable under normal conditions. Obviously a healthy person does not feel the same exigencies. Here the question of the norm comes up again. We will understand the obsessive paralysis of action and its connection with the basic disturbance only by contrasting it with the normal conditions of acting. Why, in the case of obsessives, do the minimum requirements for action exceed so much those of every day life? Or, if we reverse this question, why can a healthy person acquiesce in conditions unacceptable to the obsessive?

There is never a situation in which all reasons for an action can be surveyed, in which all consequences can be anticipated. We can never feel absolutely sure. Whatever we decide, we have to leave room in our calculations for the unknown, for the unforeseen. All actions have a tentative character. If we really demand full certainty, we have to cease acting.

A President, preparing an important message to Congress, will have many drafts made until the final version is reached. He will consult his advisers; he will test and check all possibilities. Even so, he will have to take a chance and run a risk. Ultimately all reasoning has to be brought to an end by a "fiat," as James said. It might be even more appropriate to replace the divine "fiat" by a human "sic volo." Action is necessarily always one-sided. If we move to the right we cannot move to the left. Only where there is a choice between at least two possibilities, only when we can decide, do we really act. But all objective reasons will never bring forth a final decision. The last step we have to make ourselves, following our opinion, inclination, confidence. If all has been prepared as well as possible, we have in all our actions to trust to our good luck. Action demands repose.

Under normal conditions we can act because in our sympathetic relations to the world we can rely on things and on ourselves. Like good swimmers we have trust in our strength and in the water which will carry us. Obsessives are literally not good swimmers; they see only the menacing depth. For them the water like everything else in the world, is a hostile element. The obsessive may spend an hour in mailing a letter. His fingers will not open and will not give the letter away. He cannot let it go; for the moment he drops the letter, it will be out of his reach, absorbed by the dreadful torrent of events, carried from the past now out of his control into a future equally remote from his power.

All our productions will be detached from us when they are completed. To finish something means to abandon it to the world, to trust it to its own fate. As long as I am writing a paper, it belongs to me exclusively. When the paper has been published, it continues to be my paper. However, the relation has been changed. It also belongs to the public, and I am responsible for what I have written or said. In finishing the paper I give it to the world for criticism. The results of my action over which I no longer have control work back on me. In acting we have some influence on the world, but whatever its reaction may be, hostile or friendly, critical or enthusiastic, we are at its mercy. Our surrender to the world need not be unconditional; still, in all our actions we have to deliver our work and ourselves to it. Our historical existence—not the history which we suffer, but that which we produce—is realized in relation to The Others, individuals or groups. Only as a counterpart of another being do I realize my own self. Our history begins at the moment when our actions have been detached from ourselves, just as a child first belongs to the mother when in birth it has been separated from her and has begun his own existence. "Doing" means to have done something and to have given it away. Our history does not proceed in our daydreams. Only in the process of objectivating do we produce something, which in turn determines our history. The actions of a man belong to him as his history, which he cannot revoke or undo. Our past is out of our control. We can give up the present—in other words we can act—only if we have some confidence in the world to which we deliver our work and to which we deliver ourselves through our work and actions. This is one of the reasons why the obsessive cannot act. He is unable to finish anything, or he wants to undo what he has done; for being surrounded by evil and decay he cannot permit anything of his own to escape from his control. The life of the obsessive is shaped by his defense against decay in a sequence of moments, each one limited to the present. The historical articulation of time is lost, in some cases to such a degree that "to have done" and "going to do" no longer have for the obsessive distinctive, temporal meanings. A patient may worry whether the money he has in his box at home is not the same as that which he is afraid of feeling compelled to steal just now.

In our history, part of the past remains and lasts. However, history has many more and quite different aspects. There is the past, which was once and is no longer, the story which is told in the past tense of grammar, not in the perfect tense like the history which remains. With a smile we look upon an old Chrysler model; with a similar smile we may read a letter that we wrote as a child, or we may discover our image in a faded photograph of high school graduates. Yet the viewing of the past is not always pleasant. The one who complains of losses, and the one who enjoys the progress, both consider the past from a distance.

Sometimes the distant past is suddenly revived and becomes actual again. In depressive states, the proscription is cancelled and the past resurrects as guilt of which we cannot be purged. In guilt we are overwhelmed by and chained to the past, which is known and present although it is gone. Acting alone passes; the action stays. In being performed, our deeds become irrevocable, final.

In the history which we suffer, the history which befalls us in events and relationships of our early childhood and later, the past also remains—but it remains present. In fact, as food once absorbed is turned into a part of our own bodies, those events become absorbed and persist in actual continuity. It is mainly this aspect of history that psychotherapy is concerned with, the psychotherapist trying to open up a perspective in which for the first time former events are turned into a distant past. These events do not have weight because of their uniqueness; they are not always dramatic in character; they are not "historical" events. They belong much more to the imponderables. Only because of their occurrence in the early, most plastic, periods of our lives, peculiar but banal conditions are perpetuated in our general attitudes.

There are other events, not noted in any chronicle. They belong to a group of activities which, in the routine of everyday life, do not outlive their performance. Recurrence is their mark. There is nothing which distinguishes the breakfast of today from the breakfast of tomorrow. The affairs of everyday-life routine do not enter into our histories. They do not form turning points where our lives take new and unique directions. Thus they become a matter of course, not demanding the effort, care, and concern of an important decision. We do not need deliberation because these things have been settled once and for all.

In the life of the obsessives this area of automatized routine has been completely abolished. For them everything gains the importance of an affair of state. Eating, drinking, and even breathing, are not exempted. The zone of harmless, indifferent existence has been eliminated. There is no longer any place where the obsessives feel at home, no home where they are sheltered enough to be off-guard. To act as if in historical action is the only way left open to them; but even there they can find neither a start, nor continuation, nor an end.

In a public meeting we make a deliberative speech; we select our words; we give reasons; we build up our talk as a whole. In our conversation at home we want to feel at ease. We do feel at ease if we can take up any theme and if we can start anywhere, just as we like. Among our friends we can behave in this way because we know that we are received with sympathy, and that there are no lasting consequences. We feel at ease if it does not matter that we do this and fail to do that. A bright remark, a good story, are not forbidden; but they should not be planned or prepared in advance. Planning disturbs the comfort of living at the spur of the moment, of giving ourselves completely to the present. Planning creates stiffness; vigilance causes distance.

The obsessive cannot make a start—neither a start to his own liking, nor a start based on reasons. He cannot start anywhere because he feels himself not supported by any sympathetic relations to the environment. He cannot start from reasons because reasons can never be complete. In every action we have to give some preference to one thing. Yet, in a world like that of the obsessives, where the physiognomic *entropy* has reached a maximum, where everything is as evil as the rest, nothing is inviting enough to be taken up first, nor does anything suggest the direction in which to move next. Where can someone turn who is surrounded by decay and filth? Action is possible only in a heterogeneous space where one direction is better than any other one. It becomes impossible in the homogeneous space of evil in which the obsessive lives.

The obsessive's "perfectionism" serves to overcome the paralysis of action. Action is not delayed by an extreme ambition to accomplish something perfect; perfectibility alone permits action. For only if something were perfect, i.e., faultless, and therefore immune against the attacks of decay,—only on that condition could a work be considered complete and, therefore, finally perfect in the sense of grammar.

ORDERLINESS

Like "perfectionism" obsessive orderliness belongs to the weapons of defense. But orderliness is no universal attitude of an obsessive person. While on his desk everything may be kept in finicking order, in the wastepaper basket nearby you may discover the mail of the last three months, unopened and heaped up in a terrible mess. The same obsessive who is very accurate in paying his bills may never be on time, disregarding all temporal order and accuracy.

Order and order are not the same. It is easy to understand why a factory, an office, or a store, is kept in order. In all such cases order is a means to an end. No craftsman could work who did not keep his tools in good order. A secretary keeps her desk in order, not necessarily because she is a pedant, but to be ready for quick and efficient work. The adopted order, in assigning one definite place among many possible ones to everything in use, eliminates the need for searching. It is likewise understandable that patients suffering from aphasia may exhibit a meticulous behavior. They insist, for example, that the suits in their closets be arranged in a definite way. However, the order which they demand corresponds to their impaired flexibility. They find their way only if one and the same arrangement is preserved. Any variation produces a "catastrophe reaction." (K. Goldstein).[1] If you want to preserve order, it has to be one definite order. It need not be the one chosen; thus far the choice is

[1]Cp. for example E. Haufmann, M. Rickers, Ossian Rina, K. Goldstein: Case Lanutti: *Extreme Concretization of Behavior Due to Damage of the Brain Cortex.* Psychological Monographs, ed. by J. F. Dashiell, Vol. 57, No. 4, 1944.

discretionary; but the attitude which gives preference to one arrangement over all the other possible arrangements, this attitude is not discretionary. The stubbornness of the aphasic in maintaining order is meaningful. It aids the patient to move in the restricted field of his actions.

In the orderliness of an obsessive one cannot immediately see any such reasons. He spends hours in preserving an order which seems to serve no purposes. This order certainly is also different from the order which the scientist tries to discover in nature and in the universe. Obsessive orderliness furthermore has nothing in common with that type of productive planning where the ground-plan is outlined in its main characteristics and the details left to further elaboration. For the obsessive everything has to be settled beforehand; neither will he tolerate any sketch. He gives his attention to the minutest details, and he wants to keep those details in the focus of awareness, permitting no variation. The established order has to be preserved without the slightest change. It frequently happens—as we all have observed—that obsessives can no longer enjoy the reading of books nor use them for studies because they feel compelled to follow each line in its detail. They cannot open a textbook somewhere to find an answer to a question; they have to start reading at the first page and to go on page by page, line by line, word by word, sometimes even letter by letter. The order in which the obsessive is interested is of a very peculiar type. The obsessive's peculiarities: the interest in details, the sensitivity against change, the fear of improvisation, and the need for awareness, all point the way to an understanding of the dynamics which determine obsessive orderliness.

Suppose that the captain of a ship is informed that someone is trying to smuggle himself in. What will the captain do? He will put reliable men on guard at every possible entry, and he will turn on all his searchlights in order to prevent a stowaway from slipping on board. In a similar way the obsessive turns on all searchlights of awareness. In maintaining a fixed order, reliably known in all its details, he surrounds himself with a safety zone, which the enemy cannot pass unobserved. Every change, every innovation, the slightest relaxation of vigilance, will endanger the measures of self-protection. Everywhere in the dark, behind the small illuminated area, the evils are lurking.

When we have freed ourselves from the widespread view that experiences are to be interpreted as physiological events within a body or psychological events within an individual, we are ready to understand that in all our experiences we experience ourselves in relation to the world. Within the I-world relationship we constantly build the area which is our own. The relation My-Own—The-Other is a permanent theme of all experience. The relation My-Own—The-Other has many shades. The word "My" alone has a great number of connotations. I say: my body, my hand, my life, my voice, my wife, my child, my friend, my house, my book, my country, my thoughts, my work, my name, my image, etc. Obviously my hand belongs to me in another way than my book, my friend in another way than my acquaintance. Also I belong in another way to my country than I belong to my property. In this relationship of My-Own—The-Other, there are things which are inalienable and others which are not. There are some which live and die with me and others which may become detached.

This is not the place to undertake an analysis of the meaning of the words "my" and "mine." We use these words without hesitation. We understand them sufficiently for our everyday-life conversation. But as with many other words, for example, "Now" or "Here" or "We," it is hard to give a full account of their meaning. The mere enumeration of all the combinations into which the word "my" may enter makes it clear that the relationship My-Own—The-Other is subdivided in a multiplicity of variations. Throughout, My-Own is opposite to The-Other. However, this opposition is no absolute one. My voice belongs to me; nevertheless, in speaking I hear myself; my voice is reflected back to me and thus far it is similar to a sound which originates from The-Other. We have already seen that similarly my work will not be completed until it has become objectivated. I and My-Own are also a part of the world; there is a constant exchange between myself and The-Other. It is true that "my house is my castle." But every house is on a street; there are other houses besides my own. Neighbors enter my house. If they are my friends they belong to me although they also are of The-Other. There is an invisible borderline which separates my world from The-Other. An acquaintance has his place beyond the border, a friend on this side.

In psychoses the relations which connect and separate My-Own and The-Other are basically changed. The obsessive lives as if in a beleaguered fortress; all approaches are blocked and guarded. The opposition has become an almost absolute one. There is no longer any peaceful exchange with The-Other; all friendly contacts have been severed. The obsessive is alone. In his solitariness he defends his own against attacks, which threaten him from all sides. In this struggle, orderliness is one of the means of defense.

Through order the planner enlarges the contacts with the world, the craftsman facilitates them, the aphasic patient preserves them, the obsessive severs them.

ISOLATION

There are other modes of obsessive behavior which serve the same intention. They do it in a more drastic and concrete manner. In analyzing them one does not need the metaphors that one is forced to use in discussing orderliness. If we hear that Mrs. W. wore for several weeks, day and night, the same shirt, or that Miss F. during several months never took off her pajamas, the tendency of this behavior needs not much explanation. And those cases are by no means rare. No doubt the shirt and the pajamas became dirty and filthy. In fact, Mrs. W. finally had to pull the shirt in pieces from her body. Nevertheless, the shirt or the pajamas are used in the fight against dirt, against contamination which frightens the patients. The shirt belongs to the patient like an armor. It is of her Own; even if it is soiled, it still helps to ward off the invasion of decay which comes from outside. The patient cannot change the shirt because the clean one belongs to The-Other and is, therefore, unclean.

In the development of an obsession one can well observe how the process of isolation steadily gains in power until the patient is completely alone. At the beginning the defense is directed against that which obviously belongs to The-Other. Mrs. W.

first reacted against all persons who belonged to the family of her husband. The estrangement grew. For a while she still clung to her mother, but in vain. Also in other cases patients try to keep one line of contact open; it usually is a futile attempt. After a while they fail; the person by whom they tried to hold fast is moved over into the hostile camp; he also becomes a part of The-Other, and enters the group of the untouchables.

In the great majority of cases, the relations to the therapist have no better fate. We are not surprised to find in a case report a remark like this: "tendency to absolute dissimulation." Obsessives do not dissimulate because they are more hypocritical than the rest of mankind. Frankness is a variable, its "quantities" depending on the distances which separate us from The Other. To our friends we will reveal our true selves. When the distance grows, we become more and more impersonal until we finally close the visor. The obsessive's tendency to dissimulate is a function of his complete solitariness. No communication is possible with that part of the world in which the obsessive lives all by himself. The dissimulation is no voluntary act. No other mode of behavior is left open to the obsessive. When the current gets too strong and the fuses are blown out, the patients fall into a panic. An alteration in the established order, a forced change of the protective distance, a disturbance of the ritual, all have the same effect. So does a word, spoken or written, which calls the objects of abhorrence by their proper names.

THE POWER OF THE SPOKEN AND PRINTED WORD

The effect of such words is certainly not less shocking than that of the things themselves. Against the attacks of the evil things a defense appears possible. Against the Word there is no defense. One cannot turn away from it. It follows and like a virus gets through the narrowest pores. Sound is a pursuer; it can be a persecutor. The acoustical substance in which language is formed bestows on the word a magic power to which the obsessive succumbs. But this is not the only reason. Words are more than abbreviating signs. They do not stand for individual things. They are a means of separating the essence, the "What," from individual things, and enable us to deal with the "What" itself. The word "year" comprehends as a unit the multitude of days and hours, the thousands of moments, which we experienced one to the exclusion of the other. The word "yesterday" signifies a past, which while we experienced it was present. In speaking we always transcend the immediate data. On a map we grasp at one glance the spatial structure of a country, which we can never see directly. If someone spent all his life in traveling through the U.S.A., he would pass from horizon to horizon. Nobody will ever see with his eyes the U. S. as the one whole which the map shows. By the means of symbols we break through the sensory horizon. Words, likewise, do not verbalize things or situations which we already have had before in the same way.[2] They first make it possible to separate the perennial structure of things from their accidental aspects and to deal with the totality which we perceive in particular perspectives only. Through their names things become graspable. The word, the names, open a new way of communication. In naming a thing we gain access to its "What."

In the world of magic the enunciation of names conjures up the things themselves. The word is not felt as a mere sign; in its sensory appearance, as sound, it cannot but awaken and call forth in many forms and metamorphoses the "What" to which it gives a name. In the world of magic, signification is not severed from power. Whenever a name is pronounced, the speaker has power over the thing, or he draws its power near to himself.

Even the written or printed word retains for the obsessive its magic power. Contact with the printed word "Death" etc. is contaminating. If it occurs, the patient has to go through a ritual of cleaning; after direct contact with dismal things he

[2]The nominalists interpret words as signs, even as signals, for individual things. Cp. Ogden and Richards *The Meaning of Meaning*, 4th Edition, New York, Harcourt, Brace & Co., 1936. If nominalism were consistent, words would be interpreted as signs for transitory perspectives only, not for "this pencil" but for "this pencil as I see it in this fraction of a second." The individual thing is already an identical "What" seen through many perspectives. The same is true of individual words. They are sounds pronounced at various places and moments. Through all the variations of voices, dialects, intonations, we hear the same word. The generalization, which according to nominalism should be accomplished by the signification, is in fact already hidden in the semantic sign as well as in the matter signified.

can still purge himself and restore the status quo, while the spoken word leaves him in helpless despair. These differences reflect accurately the differences of contacts that exist in the various fields of sensory modalities. The sensitivity against words in general indicates the importance of the physiognomical in obsessive experience. The patient who is at the mercy of the spoken word lives in a magic world. The power of the word by which the obsessive is overwhelmed is a magic phenomenon. However, it does not belong to the obsessive ritual; it precedes it.

THE RITUAL

It is important to realize that the obsessive lives in a world basically changed in its structure. The ritual is a counter-charm directed against the spells by which the patients are encircled. The attacking forces determine the counter-measures.

The world of magic is a primitive one in so far as physiognomies of things are interpreted as the immediate expressions of living forces animating these things and emanating from them. Sharpness, for example, is an expression of a piercing force. From the physiognomies one can directly read off the forces dwelling within them. Through the physiognomical characters the true being is revealed. This method of simple translation ascribes to the acting forces the same qualities as seen in the physiognomies. Physiognomical characters have no precise localization nor a definite delineation; this spatial indetermination is translated into an "Everywhere," the lack of definite delineation into a "Reaching beyond any distance."[3] Physiognomical qualities belong to a being as a whole; therefore, the assumption is that whatever occurs to a part also occurs to the whole. Physiognomical qualities seem to spread; they are contagious; one can participate in them. This participation, however, cannot be forced or prevented. There is no norm for a technique of participation. Magic, nevertheless, tries to enforce participation; it

[3]The physiognomic forces permeate the world. In the doctrine of the four elements a physiognomic interpretation of matter dominated occidental philosophy for many centuries. All things were explained as mixtures of the four elements: fire, water, air, and earth (soil). Yet the four elements were the result of combinations of the generic qualities of dry and moist with hot and cold, i.e., of forces directly expressed in physiognomic or at least in sensory qualities.

tries to develop a technique in the sphere of physiognomical qualities, mobilizing by conjuration helpful forces against the threatening evil powers.

Every technique demands that the right means be used at the right place, at the right time, and for the right duration. Magic follows the pattern of technique. But means, place, time, everything is determined by its physiognomical values. The right place, for example, is a crossroad, the right time midnight or the new moon; the right means are not $AgNO_3$ and NaCl, but the blood or hair of friend or foe; the right procedures are not heating, cooling, compressing to a mensurable degree, but burning, burying, devouring.

Obsessives are magicians of a brand of their own. They become adepts before they have been apprentices. Without any common instruction, without communication among themselves, they develop identical techniques. The ritual of one patient frequently resembles that of another in minute detail. They need no initiation because their ritual grows spontaneously in defense against the same dangers. Their actions are dictated—as counter-measures—by the hostile forces themselves. Sometimes this fact is easy to grasp, when, for example, a patient before starting to walk always looks for a position which guarantees that he will step forward in a direction opposite to that pointing to the cemetery. Another patient never crosses the threshold of her room at college without a certain ritual. She sets a foot down, the toes pointing away from the room of another girl whom she hates fervently. After having repeated this movement three times she can turn in any direction. A boy is compelled to sprinkle a few drops of water on the threshold; only when this libation has been spent does he feel sure enough to leave his room. In these and many other cases the threshold has the function of a magic circle, separating the sacred area from the profane. Therefore, it must not be crossed without magic precautions.

That the cleaning ceremony is a direct counter-measure needs no further explanation. If patients would give us more information than they are willing to, we probably could decipher the protective meaning of all their practices. Even so, we can penetrate into their secrets and reach an understanding of some of their attitudes in general, while details remain enigmatic. That the patient has to repeat certain actions a certain number of times—that he has chosen just these numbers—depends on events in his life history about which only the patient could tell us. However, the number ritual in general is an understandable defense mechanism.

In Frances U's life the numbers 5 and 3 played an important role. She had to touch things three times; she had to reread the last three lines on a page three times. According to her 5 was the number of the members of her family; mother, two aunts, a brother, and the patient. "Three" signified the family without the aunts, whom she hated. In another version she related 3 to the three parts of male genitalia.

For Susan M. 13 and 17 were taboo, the number 13 because it was connected with the date of her father's death, the number 17 with the death of a sister of her brother-in-law. Susan also hated the letter "D", because it was the first letter of the word "Death."

Repetition removes spontaneity and simplicity of action, which the obsessive is afraid of; through repetition actions become formalized. Repetition is cumbersome, yet numbers are finite; with a preestablished number of repetitions an end is in sight, and actions may become final. In repeating an action a number of times, one obeys an objective order and at the same time passes through an ordeal of self-castigation. In magic practice numbers are not abstract symbols. The 3, the 5, the 10, signify concrete relations with a definite physiognomy, which might be interpreted as friendly or hostile, as blessed or cursed. The obsessives, also, are led by such considerations in their choice of numbers. But frequently the chosen numbers gradually lose their wholesome charm. Multiples of the original figures will be tried, only to increase the concern whether the counting was correct, and whether every repetition was accurately performed. The exactly measured repetitions, which should help in action, will become a new obstacle; the remedy is transformed into a poison.

The obsessive ritual is throughout one of defense, or repudiation. But this defense fails because there are in the obsessive world no friendly spirits to which the obsessive can turn for support. The magic world is balanced between good and evil, between the taboo and the mana. In the obsessive world, on the other hand, a foul air pervades everything. The smell of decay sensed at one spot spreads in larger and larger circles, not losing any strength with growing distance. A patient meets a funeral car somewhere. First he avoids this section of that street. Soon he will find the street taboo in its whole length, then the neighboring streets, and the street car which passes through it; other street car lines will follow until he cannot stay any longer in that section of the town. In many cases the patients or their families change their dwellings; they move to a distant part of the town, to another town, to another country. But the evil moves along with them. There is a pestilential atmosphere, frustrating all efforts to escape.

SEXUAL BEHAVIOR

It is this atmosphere which also shapes the sexual behavior of the obsessives. In intercourse, obsessive women usually are frigid; obsessive men have to stimulate their potency through strange fantasies. Normal sexual relations neither are enjoyed nor do they play an important role in the career of obsessives. Many, if not most, obsessives of both sexes are unmarried. Obsessive women frequently substitute an infatuation for a real love into which they never enter. The physician, the brother-in-law, the fiancé of a friend, play the role of the fancied partner. Even in their imagination these patients are not able to establish direct relations. They are in need of an intermediary, a sister, a cousin, with whom they identify themselves or whom in their fancies they oust. Sister or friend nevertheless remains the guarantor of the suitability of the attachment. In some cases the patients, misinterpreting casual remarks, succeed in deceiving themselves about the interest the other person may take in them. More frequently one finds an imaginary longing for someone with whom the patients have no social contacts whatsoever.

Whenever sex occurs it appears characteristically distorted, more often obscene and fetishistic than overtly sadistic. Sex is experienced as the impure and indecent, the lewd and unchaste.

It is infected with disease and dirt. Dissociated from intimate personal relations, severed from the longing for unification, sex becomes obscene. Through the fetishistic isolation of the genitalia from the whole of the body, sexual functions are experienced as excretions and as decay.

The golden rain which floods Danaë, as in the painting by Titian, is nothing but the fecundating sperm of Zeus. From this pagan vision of sex, of divine fertility, the obsessive is far removed. He is for that reason by no means closer to Christian asceticism. If one wishes to use theological terms—and in an analysis of the basic relations of man to the world this terminology is not always inappropriate—one has to label the obsessive world as a demonic one.

Jonathan Swift has depicted it and has indulged in more than one description of sex as an execrated power. His biography leaves little doubt that he spoke from personal experience. In a poem, "The Lady's Dressing Room,"[4] he tells the story of a young lover, Strephon, who during the absence of his sweetheart steals into her room. There he finds nothing but dirt and stink. The poem gives an "inventory of all the litter as it lay." A few examples of this inventory will suffice:

"And first a dirty smock appear'd
Beneath the Arm-pits well besmear'd

. . . .

Now listen while he next produces,
The various combs for various Uses,
Fill'd up with Dirt so closely fixt,
No brush could force a way betwixt.
A Paste of Composition rare,
Sweat, Dandruff, Powder, Lead and Hair;

. . . .

But oh! it turn'd poor Strephon's Bowels,
When he beheld and smelt the Towels,
Begumm'd, besmatter'd, and beslim'd
With Dirt, and Sweat, and Ear-Wax grim'd.

. . . .

[4]*The Poems of Jonathan Swift*, Oxford, The Clarendon Press, 1937, Vol. II, p. 524 ff., with the permission of the publisher. "The Lady's Dressing Room" was first printed in 1732. The author's name was given: By the Rev. Dr. S----t. There were five reprints in the same year, followed by several more during Swift's lifetime.

The Stockings, why shou'd I expose,
Stain'd with the Marks of Stinking Toes;
O greasy Coifs and Pinners reeking,
Which Celia slept at least a Week in?"

Finally Strephon turns to "the Chest," Celia's chamber pot. "He lifts the lid." Swift compares Strephon with Epimetheus when Pandora's box is opened.

"A sudden universal Crew
Of Humane Evils upwards flew;
He still was comforted to find
That *Hope* at last remain'd behind.
. . . .
But Strephon cautious never meant
The bottom of the Pan to grope
. . . .
Thus finishing his grand Survey,
Disgusted Strephon stole away
Repeating in his amorous Fits,
Oh! Celia, Celia, Celia shits!"

In the ending stanza Swift gives an epigrammatic summary of the obsessive fascination by dirt and decay:

"But vengeance, Goddess never sleeping
Soon punish'd Strephon for his Peeping;
His foul Imagination links
Each Dame he sees with all her Stinks:
And, if unsav'ry Odours fly,
Conceivs a Lady standing by:
All Women his Description fits,
And both Idea's jump like Wits:
By vicious Fancy coupled fast,
And still appearing in Contrast."

The magnifying glass is not missing in this poem:

"The Virtues we may not let pass,
Of Celia's magnifying glass.
When frighted Strephon cast his Eye on't
It shew'd the Visage of a Gyant.
A Glass then can to Sight disclose,

The smallest Worm in Celia's Nose
And faithfully direct her Nail
To squeeze it out from Head to Tail;
For catch it nicely by the Head,
It must come out alive or dead."

In "Cassinus and Peter" and "Strephon and Chloe" Swift gave other variations of the same theme. "Strephon and Chloe" describes at length the catastrophe of a wedding night. The poem begins with praise of Chloe's charms, only to show by contrast what is hidden in every beauty. Whoever has eyes to see will discover filth as the very nature of everything.

Another passage from "Gulliver's Travels" may complete Swift's picture of human beauty:

"They [the Maids of Honor] would often strip me naked from top to toe, and lay me at full length in their bosom; wherewith I was most disgusted, because to say the truth, a very offensive smell came from their skins; which I do not mention or intend to the disadvantage of those excellent ladies for whom I have all manner of respect; but I conceive that my sense was more acute in proportion to my littleness, and that those illustrious persons were no more disagreeable to their lovers, or to each other than people of the same quality are with us. . . . They would strip themselves to the skin, and put on their smocks in my presence, while I was placed on their toilet directly before their naked bodies, which, I am sure, to me was very far from being a tempting sight, or from giving me any other emotions than those of horror and disgust. Their skins appeared so coarse and uneven, so variously coloured, when I saw them near, with a mole here and there as broad as a trencher, and hairs hanging from it thicker than packthreads, to say nothing further concerning the rest of their persons. Neither did they all scruple while I was by to discharge what they had drunk, to the quantity of at least two hogsheads, in a vessel that held above three tuns."[5]

No wonder that Gulliver collapses when returning from his last travel to the Houyhnhnms he is met by his wife, a Yahoo, who wants to embrace him.

"My wife and family received me with great surprise and joy, because they concluded me certainly dead; but I must freely confess the

[5] *A Voyage to Brobdingnag.*

sight of them filled me only with hatred, disgust, and contempt, and the more by reflecting on the near alliance I had to them. . . . And when I began to consider that by copulation with one of the Yahoo species I had become a parent of more, it struck me with the utmost shame, confusion, and horror. As soon as I entered the house, my wife took me in her arms and kissed me, at which, having not been used to the touch of that odious animal for so many years, I fell in a swoon for almost an hour."[6]

For all obsessives sex is severed from unification and procreation. Against sex in its distorted form the obsessive defenses are directed. In many cases obsessions begin early in childhood and along with them grows a monstrous apprehension of sex, manifested in queer sexual theories, in prudishness, and in illusions of erotic relations.

Grown-up women who sincerely believe that children are begotten by a mere touch need not be the victim of puritan parents. The longing for embraces, for unification, warns us that there is something else to it. Natural desire gives a presentiment of the true facts, which can anyway hardly escape attention. In the Victorian epoch, it was considered bad taste to mention anything "below the table." Yet the Victorians knew very well in private what they ignored in public. Only those will misunderstand the simple language of the body who are eager to disregard the obvious.

Bertha L., an obsessive patient, admitted to the hospital in 1916 at the age of 22, had until her 17th or 18th year the idea "that for the child to be born the woman had to be cut open."

This patient was the seventh of eight children. If she had given any consideration to this fact, or to the conditions of animal life, she would not have retained this idea. But obviously she could not give any calm consideration to sexual matters. Her "birth theory" was shaped by a deep diffidence for nature and natural events. Sex was to her a dreadful power, sexual relations acts of violence. All sexual things, therefore, appeared to her unclean. She was particularly prudish and ashamed of menstruation, which remained extremely painful for her throughout her life. A gynecological operation brought, of course, no relief. She had autoerotic fancies, which she refused to reveal in detail. She con-

[6] *A Voyage to Houyhnhnms,* Chap. XI.

fessed, however, to daydreams, "imagining dreadful things—seeing dreadful things— it was like dread all around me." She dreamed of dying and falling.

For a long time she lived in fear of sexual assault, particularly by a young man who worked with her in the same factory. The idea of assault was followed by the fear of pregnancy, which would force her to commit suicide by taking bichloride of mercury. For some time preceding her admission the patient took all food in liquid form through a glass tube in order to avoid getting bichloride in her mouth. She almost never left her house because of her fear of drugstores where bichloride was sold. "I forgot all about the fears of pregnancy and thought only of the bichloride." Nevertheless, there is little doubt that bichloride represented pregnancy, and pregnancy meant sexual intercourse—but sexual intercourse in the form of assault. Probably there was something else involved in Bertha's drinking habits. For a while she was afraid of "the tablets" in water or milk, and stopped drinking water for some time. She had, however, no fear of drinking "dark colored fluids." If she added a little chocolate to the milk, which she was hesitant to drink, she could drink it readily. A slight, but significant, change of the physiognomy was sufficient to break the spell. Obviously milk and water, and the drinking of milk and water through a glass tube, had for the patient a much more direct sexual connotation. If we explain her obsessive fear by a mechanism of substitution, we still remain on the surface. She had to suppress sexual relations, not because they were sexual, but because sex forced her into a humiliated, debased attitude. Nevertheless, it was the only role in which she could imagine herself. She could not think of herself as an equal partner. Her futile attempt to escape from sex was dominated by the distorted shape of Eros. Her fear of giving herself distorted all sexual relations, and the distorted physiognomy of sex increased her fear.

The patient blamed her mother for her troubles. Mother did not allow her to go around with young men. She was domineering and tyrannical. But the parents were quite willing to follow the advice given by the clinic. "They cooperated in every way about her going out evenings with young people and allowed her to follow her own inclinations to have a good time." Yet parental tolerance did not improve the situation. In 1921 the mother reported: "If she goes to a dance or any social gathering, she comes home exhausted and complaining of a headache and does not appear to enjoy herself at all. The family has to urge her to go." The mother added to this a quite characteristic observation: "but if it is an accident or a fire, Bertha is eager to go and does not seem upset or fatigued." The patient still refused to go with a man alone, although she went out quite often "with a crowd." At home she played games if her sister was present, but she would never stay alone in a room with her brother.

While the study of older cases has the advantage of giving valuable information about the years following hospitalization, one frequently wishes to have more data about the period preceding it.

In the case report of Bertha L. there is no further evidence that this brother during the patient's childhood or adolescence played an important role as an aggressor, or that there had ever been any actual or imaginary incestuous relations. It seems to me very improbable that Bertha's fear of being alone with her brother was caused by past events. It seems much more likely that she, in her obsessional attitude, was unable to discriminate, to see in the brother not just another male but a brother.

If the case report is deficient in that respect, there are many indications that the attitude out of which later the obsessions grew existed from early childhood on, and that the sexual obsessions were only the more spectacular ones among several others.

The patient was always considered quiet and submissive. She told herself that she had always been timid, satisfying her curiosity and dissatisfaction by fantasies and daydreams, rather than by direct questionings and contacts. She was exceedingly modest, neat, and prim. As a child she was afraid of the dark and also later on she hesitated to go any distance in the dark. Even in daytime she was afraid to go into the cellar alone.

At the age of twelve the patient would obey the mother "to the dot." "With every word I was afraid I would tell a lie; I would be afraid to answer without qualifying it; instead of saying 'it was,' I would say 'it might have been.' " Seven months after her discharge the patient was admitted for a second time. During the interval she worked as a sales girl in a department store. There she became afraid "she could not make out the customers' checks correctly; she would go into throes of indecision before submitting the check to the supervisor. She was afraid to trust herself near fine silks or goods for fear she would cut them or damage them." After the second discharge she resumed her work as a sales girl. "She felt just as bad as when she was in the hospital, except that she worked and would not quit working for anything."

In 1938, twenty-two years after her first admission, the patient lived with an older sister in a house the family had owned for forty years. The combined earnings of the two women were just sufficient to keep up the house. The sister considered the patient "about 100% improved." "She is very religious—a Catholic—goes to church once every day. She was 'always the worrying type' but seems not to be bothered any more by phobias, at least does not express any." The patient was still very sensitive about her two admissions to the Phipps Clinic. She had many friends, but never a serious love affair. She did much crocheting. For sixteen years she had held the same position as a sales girl in one of the large department stores.

Thus finally the patient had come to make peace with the world. She succeeded in fencing in her existence in a small protected area, in avoiding invalidism, and in continuing her life in an undramatic routine where day followed day without any change, without any event. For sixteen years—the years from 1922 to 1938—the patient stood at the same counter; for sixteen years she went on crocheting: a standstill of personal history in the turmoil of time.

When we see the patient in her forty-fourth year, she still is the same timid, submissive girl. She cannot take any initiative; she cannot do more than stoop in order not to be blown over. She was running away from sex, as she was running away from every other situation in which any fateful decision could be expected. In running away she turned her head backward; she was curious, liked to peep, to experience as a spectator what others actually did. "Running away" is no metaphorical term in her case.

During the summer between her two admissions the patient went to a summer resort. "There she had interchanged glances with a man who seemed all right, but when he later asked her to go to some place with him, she was upset by his advance and refused to accompany him. She later met him at the beach; he asked her to come into the water with him, whereupon she fled. He grabbed hold of her arm and tried to detain her. There was no improper suggestion, but her fancies leaped immediately to assault. The following last two days of her vacation she remained in her room, kept fearing that she would see this man. She continually thought of suicide."

Bertha L.'s case is a mild one. If in her later years she had been in treatment, her case would probably be listed as a success. Her case is a milder one because to her the world has more the character of violence than of decomposition. In classical mythology, Pan frightens the girls with his laughter. The power of Pan—the name says it—permeates the universe. This phallic god is an impertinent aggressor, but, resounding the joys of life—as his laughter indicates—, he is no monster. Sex turned our patient into a panic flight. Although she was frightened by its violent aggression, she still could realize it in some degree to be a natural power, not destructive throughout. Our patient could keep up some contacts with the world. In a crowd she felt secure; there nothing serious could happen. She did not have to emerge as an individual person who had to face her own destiny. There she felt at ease as long as, with fun and jokes, the group was moving in a circle. In the crowd she could continue her life as an anonymous being, as incorporeal as a shadow.

Masochism, which played such an important role in Bertha L.'s life, is no partial drive, neither a normal one nor a perverted one. There are no partial drives. A person is masochistic; and he is masochistic throughout, in all his relations to the world. Masochism is a specific expression—in the sexual sphere—of a basic and general attitude. Through this attitude the world gains the physiognomy of grim violence. The masochist cannot stand it to be upright as anybody's peer; only on his knees, humiliated, can he present himself as just good enough to absorb the excreta of the others.

AVARICE

Avarice, which together with orderliness and stubbornness is supposed to form the triad of the "anal character," is not very often observed in obsessive patients. The simple reason probably is that among the obsessives there are many poor ones; and only one who owns something that he could spend can overtly prove a miser. Still, obsessives are sometimes avaricious.

Every year newspapers report that, after the death of someone who had spent his life in the greatest poverty, thousands of dollars were found in his wretched room. These are the true misers, not those who hate to give to others, but those who do not allow themselves to use any of their property for themselves. To use something means to use it up. From day to day one can see how it is dwindling more and more. In the case of money, the loss is especially to be felt. Money is reified potentiality. When you go down town with a few hundred dollars in your pocket, you can buy numberless things—potentially—that is only as long as you have not yet bought anything; the moment you have spent your money, all of its potentiality is lost. Instead of the infinite potentiality you own now only one thing in reality. Returning from the city you are not only poorer for as much as the amount actually spent, but for all the potentialities you have lost. The miser, who is aware only of the process of dwindling, for fear of consumption starves to death in the midst of his wealth. The skotoma for growth and rejuvenation and the sensitivity for consumption and passing away form the link between avarice and obsession. Obsessives are not only, and not always, economical with things and with money. There are other conditions when patients are seized by the panic fear of the passing and fading. Sex is one of them and time another. The half truth, "omne animal post coitum triste," is true for many of the obsessives. They are "tristis" even "ante coitum." In every sexual activity they experience nothing but the loss; they anticipate it and fight it before it happens.

Others, incapable of accomplishing any meaningful action, are compelled to give their attention to the irresistible flow of time, to register moment after moment ticking away in a horrifying emptiness.

Annette M., a patient I have mentioned before, complained that for the last two years preceding her admission "she felt that she could not get well and now she cannot stand to have a clock tick; she had a fear of death and begrudged each second." She could not stand to hear people say they were "looking forward" to anything; she wanted "to hang on to the minutes, for she felt she had to die and she did not want to lose a minute." She was terrified if people spoke quickly. "Oh! It gives that awful fear, just as if I were in a runaway, as if something would surely happen—I feel as if I were not alive, and I stop to think and take hold of things to realize that I am still alive."

The patient "has simply been permeated with fear and horror." "It seems that all the bad things have taken control." She saw death all around herself. There was a store where a woman, who had died two years before, used to shop. Annette refused to go there. She could not read books written by dead people. She was afraid of wearing a certain pair of shoes because the preceding summer she walked in them over a road where a hearse had passed. When she visited a family named Sp. she could not touch the picture of D. Sp., who had died sometime before. She warned her mother—about whom she worried the most—about having D. Sp's daughter as a help in her house. "Be *sure,*" she wrote, "if it is quite *all right* to have Mary Sp. for the serving. You know what I mean—it was part of the scare." In a post-script to the very short letter she repeats, "Be *sure* it is all right about Mary." One could extend this list into the infinite because everything which had the physiognomy of death was frightening and almost everything could show this physiognomy. Where is the road over which not once has a hearse passed?

The patient spoke of her fear of contamination as entirely traceable to a constant terror of dying and of all connections with the trappings of death. One day she became panic-stricken because another patient placed one of Annette's skirts on a bed in the ward. The patient lay awake several hours at night feeling that she could never touch the skirt again because she was sure that someone had died in that bed. For several years she would not eat dried beef because it made her think of something dead. Likewise, another obsessive patient reported that "she was disgusted by everybody who was old. In former days, she had not the heart to send a beggar from her door. Now she could not even bear to see an old man's hand."

The words "it made her think of something dead" suggest that the fear is aroused by an association of ideas. But the patients do not think of death as much as they feel its immediate presence. They are afraid of a sensory contact with death, which permeates everything around them. Annette, "for example, could not touch a newspaper for fear her hand or garments were touching the obituary column."

The idea of immortality was a counterpoint to Annette M.'s fear of death. If the soul did not exist after death, she thought, people were machines of whose existence one could be certain only by touching or feeling them. "As she looked at people they seemed to fade away before her eyes." Annette described her experience of depersonalization in very characteristic terms: "I am like a deaf person in a concert." She asked for proofs of immortality, for absolute proofs. She thought that she could believe in immortality "if she could see it under the microscope or through a telescope." She combined the magic techniques of warding off death with pseudo-scientific methods of proving life. For a while the patient was interested in getting employment in a chemical or some other scientific laboratory. She probably dreamed of replacing her sister and being near to her brother-in-law, for whom she had an infatuated love. But there was also the hope "that some day science will be able to create life either chemically or through some zoological discovery." Life, which could not be realized in sympathetic co-existence, should be obtained by the forces of technical procedures. Annette had the "vague belief that chemistry or zoology may create life, and hence eventually control the powers which destroy it."

IV

CLINICAL VARIETIES AND THEIR PATHOGENESIS

IN THE PRECEDING DISCUSSION we have tried to understand obsessions as the behavior of obsessives, i.e., of persons living in a world deeply altered from the world familiar to us. Our main concern has been to grasp the intrinsic unity of the manifold symptoms, and their relations to each other and to a basic disturbance.[1] The etiology, the pathogenesis, the development of the disease from an early unostentatious beginning to the annihilation of a meaningful existence, the motives and ends which may perhaps determine such a fatal development, all these problems have not yet been considered. An analysis of the structure of a mental disease, although it gives no direct answer as to its origin, does so by innuendo. It provides certain criteria which supplement the methods of clinical observation and description and of genetic hermeneutics and interpretation. The three methods do not exclude each other; just the opposite, each requires the others for its completion. In using one of them we tacitly presuppose or refer to information obtained by the others.

In the past the biographic method concerned with the single case became more and more dominating, almost to the exclusion of clinical observation based on a comparison of many cases. But the single case as such is incomprehensible. In every study of a single case we cannot but use general psychopathological principles and general clinical experience. We understand the single case, or better the individual person, as one realization of man in general, of his capacities and limitations. In practice a single case may provide the occasion for investigating the general structure. The results of this procedure still will have to be checked by their application to other cases. In the end we can

[1]Cp. E. Minkowski: *Le Temps Vécu,* Paris 1933. In this book Minkowski gives an excellent discussion of "La Notion du Trouble Générateur et L'Analyse Structurale des Troubles Mentaux," p. 207-254.

hope to obtain criteria for evaluating the factors which determine the genetic context.[2]

a. OBSESSIVE PSYCHOSES AND OBSESSIVE NEUROSES

In a survey of patients hospitalized for obsession one easily discovers a number of different developments. While there is sometimes a surprising coincidence between the cases of one group, the groups themselves show clearly marked differences. From a central group, to which our structural analysis is applicable, a case like the following one clearly detaches itself.

H. C. F., a young man, 28, married, father of two children, a traveling salesman, entered the clinic on the advice of the wife of his employer for whom he had been working since his thirteenth year.[3] "Doctor," he said on his admission, "the only thing that seems to be troubling me is that I imagine that I am going to harm myself. At first I imagined that my little baby was going to die and that I would be the cause of it." Asked how he felt now he answered, "I just feel that I would harm myself. My ambition is not to do this thing, but it seems as though some power is driving me, is constantly making me think of this thing. I am Roman Catholic, and I believe that if I should commit suicide having my full senses I would go to hell. Here I feel safer. I came here with the intention to be cured, and I know I am going to be cured." The idea to kill his baby came to him suddenly on a business trip to the south. He gave the exact date, June 2. The day before, a Sunday, he went to a show with a girl. "I fooled around with this girl Friday and Sunday night." On Sunday he came back alone to the hotel "having left her disgustedly because I thought I ought to have been with better company, and because she had deceived me." By that he meant that she had told him the night before that she had had sexual relations with a friend of his, Tom, who was away from New Orleans that day. Patient was "surprised, possibly a little jealous and disgusted that this girl had been with this fellow. He was surprised also that this fellow (Tom) would be untrue to his wife, who was true to him. 'I thought that day that it was an awful thing of him.' " F. had been married for 8 years. The first child was born after five years of marriage. At the time of the onset of his compulsive thoughts, his wife was pregnant again. The second child was unwanted. The patient did not know of any

[2]Cp. L. Binswanger: *Der Fall Ellen West,* L.C.

[3]C. Flournoy has published this case in the *Johns Hopkins Bulletin,* Vol. XXV, p. 328-330, 1914.

reason why they had no children during the first years of their marriage. They did not use contraceptives.

His wife came from a family of somewhat higher social level. F. had known his wife for about five months before they were married. During that time they sometimes had intercourse. "After we were married we always regretted it." Two or three months before they were married his wife became pregnant; she went to see a doctor who performed an abortion. The patient in telling this story was very strongly affected by sadness and shame—blushed and wept. "I feel tonight that I would sooner die than have another abortion performed. I have practically committed a murder." He nourished a suspicion that someone else might have been the father. "If it had been someone else's fault," he thought, he "would not have to answer to God for this sin." He was very jealous and suspected the faith of his wife on many occasions.

Before he married, since his seventeenth year he had many sexual relations with "fast women." During the months of his engagement he did not stop these relations. After marriage his job gave him many opportunities to continue his old habits. It seems, however, that he never went the full way, although he liked to "fool around" with easily acquiescing girls.

H. C. F. was a travelling salesman by temperament,—quick, talkative, easy-going, adaptable, industrious. While he might have foresworn song, it was hard for him to give up wine and women. Obviously, he was still too young for marriage at the time he married. His jealousy indicated that a distance remained between him and his wife, a disinclination, perhaps directed more against the institution of marriage than against the person he had married. Jealousy also served him as an excuse to blame his wife for his own faults and to persecute in her the sins he wanted, but did not dare, to commit. For he also liked to see himself as an honest, reliable fellow, obedient to the tenets of the Church. H. C. F.'s jealousy had still another source. He was in need of a third person in order to arouse his own interest. This was so when he met his wife for the first time, when he courted her, and also after marriage. One may think of a repetition of the "Oedipus-triangle." Yet the other one for H. C. F. was not the rival whom he found blocking his way; just the opposite, the other one pointed the way H. C. F. could take for himself. In his relation to the New Orleans girl, Tom, the patient's friend, was no competitor. The girl was quite willing to serve both gentlemen. While H. C. F. frowned at Tom's adventures, he envied him. He had come to realize what another married man had done in his place, and he could not forget it. Docile by training and by nature he first had to learn what one does and what not. His appetite came when others ate.

During his stay at the clinic, where he was always cooperative, it was made clear to him that his obsessions arose "out of conflicts due to desire (1) to be absolved from the sin of abortion, (2) for extra-marital relations and sexual freedom, and (3) domination desires regarding his wife whose social superiority he resented."

He was discharged two months after admission "in excellent physical condition, cheerful, and optimistic. Had quite consistent self-control."

Differential Diagnosis

The differences between this patient and the obsessives who fight contamination are striking. While there was, in the third decade of H. C. F.'s life, a sudden onset of compulsive thoughts, an abrupt, dramatic manifestation of a smothering conflict, successfully and definitely treated in a short time, we find in the other group a continuous development from an early, unostentatious start to a final, calamitous state of invalidism. At least this is the rule in the majority of cases that have ever been in need of hospital treatment. As these patients dislike to give a correct description of their disease, the information obtained during the first interview is frequently misleading. Sometimes the patients pick out the most disturbing symptoms, discounting the less obtrusive ones, but more often they simply conceal what they really know. Only gradually the true story seeps through.

Regarding H. C. F. his mother said that he was a healthy child. "Always was bright; he was at the head of his class usually and made other boys jealous. He loved school. Always wanted his own way, liked *outdoor* games; very obedient at home, especially towards his father. Always lived at home until he got married. The father was rather strict and particular; his children couldn't stay out later than eight o'clock in winter and nine in summer. After that, they had to learn their lessons. Patient never fussed about that with his father; knew he had to do it. The three children always agreed. Patient was sixteen or seventeen years old when for the first time he danced at school. Was crazy about dancing, but his father didn't like it. Married at twenty. Was never seclusive; had a lot of friends, boys and girls. Patient has always been quick tempered; his wife is more quiet, and does not talk; the whole family of his wife, except the mother, are not talkative at all."

We do not expect to hear a report of that kind in a contamination case. We may briefly compare this with another case picked at random. It is the case of a woman, M. H., who, in 1923, at the age of thirty-three, was admitted to the clinic in panic over the possibility that "clothing and everything which has come in contact with patient was contaminated by a douche medicine spilled in 1915." Her obsessions began in the tenth year. At that age she feared her mother would die; she would start two or three times for school and return to reassure herself that her mother was alive. She was reliable and bright; completed the eighth grade at the age of fourteen. She was sensitive and timid; devoted all her energies to her work, and made no friends. Throughout childhood and adolescence she had many obsessive fears and phobias, until towards her twentieth year the fear of contamination became dominating.

This case is different from H. C. F.'s as much in the end as in the beginning.

In the contamination group special tensions grow up with the entrance into the clinic, if not earlier. M. H. was herself anxious to be admitted to the hospital, but "she was no sooner admitted than she became panic-stricken about being there." The relations to nurses and to other patients do not remain unaffected for long. In almost all case records one feels an antagonism between the doctor and his patients, who complain and quarrel, and who are at the same time obtrusive and reticent. It will not be long until the hospital or the psychotherapist are included in the long list of those whom the patients blame for their troubles. After discharge, therefore, the patients rarely keep up friendly relations with the hospital; they are eager later on to forget their hospitalization, or at least hope to have it kept secret.

M. H., when visited by a social worker, was quite "embarrassed, and flushed deeply when worker referred to her old feeling of contamination." She explained that she felt uncomfortable telling of her past illness in the office for fear someone might hear her through the partitions of her office. On the other hand, the social worker who went to see H. C. F. eight years after his discharge "attempted to make the conversation private, but there is apparently no selfconsciousness nor sensitiveness on the part of the patient." H. C. F. promised to come for an interview, and he came; M. H. also promised to come for an interview but never did. Although she spoke "pleasantly of The Phipps Clinic," she did not corroborate her words by her actions.

She also told the social worker that she "at present is getting along very well." A letter from her physician written fourteen and a half years after the patient's discharge from the hospital shows how this somewhat ambiguous information has to be evaluated.

After her discharge from the hospital, M. H. had psychoanalytic treatment for more than six years, and later kept in touch with her psychoanalyst, who at the patient's age of forty-eight reported: "Her psychiatric condition has shown fluctuation. From a short period after the operation until about a year ago she had the best mental health which I have ever seen in her. Her compulsions were very much reduced—she held one position and was able to live more comfortably than ever before. Her anxiety at that time centered in her fear of the recurrence of her carcinoma and she was decidedly hypochondriacal and required frequent reassurance from her medical man. In the past year, however, she has become very upset again, is several hundred dollars in debt because of extravagances of cleaning and moving from place to place because of her contamination fears. During the past summer she was close to hospitalization, but seems to be improving at the present time. I do not know whether she kept her job. . . ."

When H. C. F. was seen eight years after his discharge, he had gone in business for himself two years before and had been very successful. To the interview he came "an immaculately dressed, prosperous appearing man. . . . He talks eagerly and a little tensely, is very anxious for the doctor to know that he is now entirely well. . . . In general, he has the bluff, good-fellow attitude of the traveling salesman." He had only the greatest cordiality toward the Clinic, and said "he feels it was a wonderful experience for him and that he has been much more stable since." At times he was a little sensitive about it and would "try to put it out of his mind" that he had been there. But he remembered that he had been told that that was a bad business and bred future trouble, and besides he asked himself if there was really anything to be ashamed of. He certainly betrayed no sign of sensitivity at that time. He asked heartily for various patients and said he must admit that after all he had had many good times there. "Immediately after leaving the Clinic he sometimes had the same old thoughts, but they had lost their sting—were more like memories. Gradually the periods of recurrence of these thoughts became less and less frequent, and now they have disappeared. He has sometimes wondered whether, if things went badly, he would again have obsessions. But on the whole he feels that he has been fairly well tested in the past eight years, and that he is assured of the permanence of his relief. Last summer his wife had a ruptured tubal pregnancy and while distressed about her condition and danger, he thinks he reacted quite normally to it. For a year or two after leaving the Clinic he was timid about undertaking new things; bought an automobile and was afraid to drive it etc.; but he has gotten over this. When asked what had helped him most, he says it was certainly Dr. F's making him argue things out, and see through them. "Eight million times he must have told me 'reason it out,' and made me do it. . . . You haven't any idea what that has done for me—just making me think things out and not get into a huff about them." He feels he learned to do the best he could and to be satisfied with that, rather than getting mad about not doing better, as a result of which his days go much more smoothly. He outlined his case in brief to the interviewer, and seemed to have a good grasp of the mechanism." As H. C. F. died four years later from typhoid fever, there are no more recent reports.

Turning from a case of obsessive psychosis[4] to one of compulsive thoughts of killing, one feels as if one were leaving a greenhouse with tropical plants and entering one in which cyclamen or azaleas are in bloom. The atmosphere and colors are different throughout. This difference is perhaps nowhere more obvious than in the manifest symptomatology of each group. H. C. F. fights against impulses of which he morally deeply disapproves. Both the impulse, with its unconscious motives, and the disap-

[4]I introduce here a term used occasionally by Dr. J. C. Whitehorn in our staff meetings at The Henry Phipps Clinic.

proval belong to the patient himself. The theme of H. C. F.'s compulsion is a definite, concrete, future action. His homicidal impulse is directed toward a definite goal, first against his child, later against himself. With this intention the patient tries to break through one definite situation which has become intolerable to him. With the exception of this peculiar difficulty, his relations to the world and his interpersonal relations remain intact. His obsessive neurosis does not originate in a basically distorted world nor does it change for him the common structure of the world.

M. H., however, felt she must go to Washington to buy clothes because all Baltimore was contaminated. "When the patient's landlady turned the matting on the floor of her bedroom, M. H. thought some of her soiled clothes might have been on the floor and perhaps some wax (leucorrheal discharge) might have got on the floor. She first felt she could not wear any clothes which were out in the room at the time. Then the fear spread to all of her clothes; she was unable to sleep in the room again—went to the Y.W.C.A. Then she began to buy new clothes; felt she could not visit any of her friends because she might have a contamination and then she would never be able to go back again. She began to bathe constantly, even to wash hair constantly, to buy new clothes, to wear them once and to buy other ones. Moreover, every store in which she bought clothes became contaminated. As all Baltimore was contaminated, she planned to go to Washington for new clothes. She felt if she could bathe her entire body and wash her hair in one room, then step naked into a new room with all new clothes, then go away from the city, she might get rid of the fear. She had bathed until she had made her body sore with scrubbing."

M. H. does not feel compelled to one single action with a definite goal, realizable in the future; she fights the evil which is omnipresent within and beyond the visible horizon, but which is an ungraspable and therefore irresistible potentiality. M. H. is condemned to carry on without interruption a hopeless struggle. She is not confronted with a conflict between a desire and a moral command, but exhausts herself in a fight against decay, against evil as a metaphysical substance.

I speak about metaphysical experience, and I really mean what I say. The senses are metaphysical organs. They do not know any skepticism; no Cartesian doubt has been impinged upon them. Through our senses we experience reality. Philosophical reflection may cast doubt upon the truth of this experience. However, this afterthought does not alter at all the character of sensory experience. In everyday life, whether we are philosophers or not, the senses reveal to us "being," a world coexisting with us, and therefore not ordered in a neutral scheme, but related to us as living beings. In this relationship all things are endowed with physiognomies, attractive or repulsive, useful or harmful, good or evil. Even though sensory experience be deceptive and illusory, on this illusion then all our everyday life is based. It is in this area also that we are confronted with mental disturbances. The basic structure of the everyday-life world provides the frame of reference in relation to which we actually distinguish between strange and normal behavior. Unfortunately, and to the great disadvantage of psychiatry, the order of the everyday-life world and our experience of this order has been subjected—since the beginning of our modern era— to an interpretation for which mathematical physics presented the model. Only when we emancipate ourselves from the bias of this interpretation will we be able to understand in theory the order on which we base in practice our psychiatric judgment.

Further Differentiations: The Contaminated and the Contaminator

The following case may serve as an example of a third group of obsessions, different in some respects from the two other groups, but closer to the contamination-obsession.

A. G., thirty-seven, married, father of three children, Scotch Presbyterian minister, worried since his fourteenth year about "three branches of thinking": 1. that he might cheat someone; 2. that he might get things dishonestly; 3. that he might poison someone. In any money deal—paying of a bill or street car fares, drawing of checks—he always felt that he cheated some other man. He felt so disgusted that he never told anybody, not even his wife. His wife, however, wrote in a letter about his peculiar habit of staring at a piece of money. "If he gives me any amount, he will ask over and over again how much he has given me." In buying things the patient always felt that he gave too little money and that the clerk gave him too much change. In the clinic he once had to pay for some glasses. The bill was not clearly written and seemed to be either $1.00 or $1.50. To be prepared for both alternatives, A. G. carried a one dollar bill and two quarters. He asked the saleswoman how much he owed her. She replied, "One dollar." The patient repeated, "One dollar?" The girl answered, "Yes." Then the patient put his hand in his pocket, drew out a one dollar bill, and looked at it three or four times to make sure it was a one dollar bill. "Then," the patient said, "I threw it down on the table and looked at it again when it was lying there. She said, 'That is right.' I said, 'Is that right?' She answered, 'Quite correct.' " "I generally worry," he added, "about a thing like this until a new one pushes it out of my mind. If you had not called for me, I think I would have worried all afternoon." He was very much worried about the episode; he had no explanation except that he did not recall the woman picking up the dollar.

As a schoolboy he would worry before examinations that he might be dishonest, and afterwards that he had been dishonest. "The first concrete incident occurred at fifteen, when taking a Latin examination. We had a little snatch of an examination. We had the word *iter* to decline. I was not sure of the genitive case. It happened that this word occurred in a sentence to be translated. Now, someone asked the teacher if it was right to look up this word. He said no. I looked anyway and got it right. I won the highest honor in the school and was given a scholarship with about $100.00. This was one point of a set of final and intermediate examinations, and I could not get rid of the feeling that this point possibly might have had something to do with it."

When he reads a newspaper or a magazine he always has the feeling that he will receive some illegitimate aid on the examinations which he has passed years ago. The most recent was twelve years before his admission. "I argue to myself like this. This building (Phipps Clinic) was not built when that happened, or this paper, or this book not printed when that happened. Then I look to see when it was published, or I overcome it with a great deal of pressure. Sometimes it makes me feel very depressed. They are rational arguments, but they ought not to be necessary."

The feeling of poisoning someone was not so strong. "I feel that there might be some poison in the cup; through some inscrutable way I have left poison in the cup after having taken it from the table dish. I never feel this way about the dishes or cups of other people, or the general dishes. I never have anything on my person to put in the cups, but I cannot get rid of the feeling that I have left something in the cup which someone else will drink. Like a servant might chance to drink what is left in the cup. I have never felt that any particular person might drink it. I have had this feeling before my marriage. . . . I have tried by the dint of will power to prove the absurdity of these things. I succeed for a while, but the case comes right back, and I am unable intellectually to convince myself."

Towards the end of his stay at the hospital, A. G. wrote a long letter of confession. In this letter he gave to his wife, who was five years older than he, an endless list of all "the sins" he had committed. Although he accused himself severely, one does not get the impression of a deep regret, much more of an enjoyment in his role of a sinner. The letter, which was never mailed, was written in a smooth, elaborate manner: "These sins, this unbroken stream of sins, which runs down from my early boyhood days, from the time when I was ten years of age or thereabouts, are all of the same general nature, are all of a sexual origin. They differ somewhat in degree, but they are alike in kind. The exceedingly sinful sin which I have described above is not the only one of which I have been guilty since our marriage. Only last winter on one occasion, and on another occasion when we lived in the faculty house in Richmond, as horrible and as tremendous as it unquestionably was, I actually tried to have sexual connection with a hen! What do you think of that? What must every right thinking person think of that? Nor were these isolated instances. On a number of occasions, when I was a boy, before I was sixteen, in Richmond and at Warrenton, I not only tried to, but I actually succeeded in having sexual connections with hens. Oh! the shame of it! And several times, a number of times—once shortly before we were married—I was guilty of similar sinful tendencies, though not of actual connection, with a bitch and with mares! You will tnink me a 'moral quagmire,' and certainly in these respects I deserve so to be thought of."

The writer seems to be more interested in the eloquent style of his presentation than in the matter presented. In another passage of this letter, which fills, in all, more than fifteen typewritten pages, he says, "Now this horrible sin is the most recent, and in many ways the greatest sin of my life. But it does not stand alone by any means. In fact, it is but the logical and almost inevitable outgrowth of a long and persistent series of sins of a similar nature. I have been tremendously startled and mortified as I have been brought face to face with them here, as I had never been brave enough to compel myself to face them before. I cannot say that I have been unaware of them; such would have been impossible; but I have kept myself, and I might say almost or quite deliberately, as unaware of them as it was possible for me to keep myself. In other words, because it suited me best to do so, because I wanted to do so, I simply turned my back upon them and refused to weigh their gravity. If I had faced them squarely, I would have been compelled to give them up, and I simply did not want to give them up. That is the truth in this connection in a nut-shell!"

He described in detail the many relations he had with other women. They all have one thing in common: he never went the whole way; he "did not commit adultery." Towards the end of his letter he uses with great ease the knowledge just acquired in the hospital. He tells his wife that his obsessions have served him as self-punishment. "All this suffering I have, no doubt, deserved richly and fully though it has not come in the natural channel. If I had only allowed it to come in the natural channel, the channel of my real sins, it would have caused me to stop those particular sins, and then it would not have manifested itself in these unnatural channels. But, as matters have actually been, simply because I would not and did not punish myself where I should have done so, I have been compelled to punish myself elsewhere and where I should not have done so. Refusing to be normal I have had to be abnormal! In other words, in these three lines of my obsessions, *I have punished myself; I have obsessed myself, and seemingly inevitably;*— that is, my self-punishment along these lines was inevitable as I had refused to place the proper punishment on the real and actual sins."

He ends his glib confession in these two paragraphs: "There is no more that I need add now. I hope God will forgive me. I hope you will forgive me, though I realize in part how greatly I have sinned against you, and how much I am asking when I ask your forgiveness. And I do hope, finally, that my self-inflicted punishment will cease now that I have been brought face to face with its first cause. . . . Let me hear from you as soon as possible, and write fully and frankly. I trust this confession will not crush you. I shall be a different man in the future. *I do love you now.* Devotedly, your husband."

It is not clear whether A. G. had at any time a sincere intention to mail this letter. It is not even sure in how far his confessions were true, concealing, or exaggerated. It may be that, in a kind of daydreaming, he indulged in his role as a rueful sinner, and that this penance gave him opportunity to perform, with full gratification, these pseudo-acted "sins" which he had never actually committed. In all the length of this complacent narration there is no place where the patient expresses any genuine feeling for his wife. The letter shows his personal isolation and impassibility. When he entered the clinic he came from a hospital where his son was operated on for severe burns. A. G. was not in the least worried. "It makes me feel like kicking myself because I do not worry very much about that."

The patient's hope that his "self-inflicted punishment would cease" was never fulfilled. In his discharge note it is mentioned when he paid his bill he continued his worries about the correctness of his transactions. He counted the money returned to him with evident uneasiness. The nurse thought he was absent-minded. An inquiry about A. G.'s condition was returned unclaimed in 1937.

A. G.'s "conflicts" are similar to those of H. C. F. in so far as they are centered around ethical problems. The patient wants to see himself as a man who cannot measure up to his own high ideals. Somewhat timid and hesitant—this is his own explanation—he can neither approve his desires nor successfully renounce them. He sticks fast between doing and not-doing. He does not come to an action which he can either accept as his own or purge himself from afterwards. The undone actions recur in the guise of obsessions.

Differences in the Experience of Time

The differences between the two cases, however, are still more marked. A. G. does not fight against actions with a precise goal, which he fears—although compelled—to perform as his own deeds sometime in the future. A. G. worries about something he may have done. He worries about actions which may have occurred in the past. He does not know whether this vague something has been done or not. He worries about possibilities which are as ungraspable and unverifiable as the germs or the dirt in the cases of contamination obsessive psychoses. H. C. F. resists single actions, reprehensible for definite ethical reasons; they are specified and forbidden by the penal code or the canon law. If he killed his child he would be sentenced for this specific crime. A. G. is on a constant search for an indefinite wrong, which, if it had been performed, would have been nothing but an expansion of a personal state of evil that he finds in himself, of an evil being, not of an immoral action.

The fact that A. G. worries about dishonest information he may gain from reading a newspaper years after having passed an examination shows that the normal temporal structure of action is not applicable to his case. One may assume that he goes through a kind of daydreaming which provides some masochistic pleasure for him. But when we learn how he tries to reason himself out of this situation and how he fails, this assumption becomes untenable. Although he makes it clear to himself that he reads the newspaper in the Phipps Clinic, therefore not at the place of the examination but years later, all such arguments do not help to dispel the obsession. Obviously, for this type of obsessions—A. G.'s case is not an isolated one—the rational order of time, the actual relations of earlier and later, have lost their meaning. Such patients are aware of an evil which exists in themselves as a permanent substance of being, untouched by the current of time. As an omnipresent potentiality (*dynamis*) it scorns every attempt to localize it and confine it to a single moment.

The so-called "Omnipotence of Thoughts"

An "omnipotence of thought" has frequently been mentioned as a peculiarity of obsessive thinking. This power, however, is one which the patients neither enjoy nor are free to exercise at will. There is, for example, a patient who when passing a funeral home thinks of her sister's death. In fact she feels herself overwhelmed by this thought, or, more correctly, by this desire. She worries that this bad wish may really kill the sister. She has therefore to return to the funeral home and wait, sometimes for hours, until a real desire for her sister's survival arises. Of course, she could at any time think and even wish that her sister should not die. But this thought does not help as long as it is not experienced with the same unrestrained energy and, therefore, reality which gave power to the first wish. The patients are by no means free to produce the thoughts the magic power of which they fear and try to counteract. The magic power is restricted to evil thoughts which come into the mind, uncalled for, whether the patients want them or not. The evil thoughts have power over the patients; nevertheless, the patients experience them as their own thoughts and wishes for which they feel responsible. Obsessives never have the experience that by the power of their thoughts they can stop the sun in its course, or even prevent a top from spinning around. A statement that an obsessive is "an individual who has an uncommon faith in the 'omnipotence of thought,' who acts as if he could accomplish things solely by thinking of them"[5] seems to me a cruel irony. Such a statement is a rash generalization, built on an insufficient observation of the "surface phenomena," a biased interpretation of facts invented for the sake of a certain theory. The obsessives have—in their own experience—no power of thought at their disposal. They do not think; "it" thinks within them. There is an ill fate emanating from them, tied up with everything which is theirs: thoughts, actions, property. Susan M. worries that some of her belongings pass into someone else's hands and, thereby carry disease and death to the new owner, especially to her mother. The patients discover in themselves a fountain of evils which, flowing by itself, inundates their thinking and acting. Evil, as the substance of their existence, emerges in events which nevertheless they cannot but accept as their own actions.

Prognosis

The diversity of the different groups found by structural analysis is confirmed by their clinical progress. In the psychotic cases, the prognosis is usually very grave, even if one discounts those cases which later develop clearly schizophrenic symptoms. Although there are periods of relaxation, full recovery is extremely rare, whatever methods of therapy have been used. Some patients, in spite of the persistence of their obsessions manage to hold a job. The tendency toward concealment frequently grows stronger with age. In some reports considerable improvement is mentioned, an impression probably caused by the increasing skill of the patients in hiding their difficulties from even the closest observers.

However, it seems that sometimes, although the symptoms do not completely disappear, the patients are less molested by

[5]S. E. Jelliffe and W. A. White: *Diseases of the Nervous System*, Lea and Febiger, Philadelphia, 1935, p. 930. With permission of the publisher.

them. The following report illustrates how difficult it is to evaluate the degree of improvement.

In January 1919, a social worker visited the home of a patient, Miss Ella H., who in 1913, at the age of thirty-five, had been admitted to the hospital. According to her sister's report, the patient was entirely recovered. "She helped in the home and was effective as ever. Some months after leaving the hospital the patient was quite unwell—she lost weight, was sleepless, and seemed much agitated. This condition continued for four or five months; then patient began to improve, and from that time up to the present showed no symptoms of her old trouble." The patient's sister impressed the social worker as being reserved and unwilling to talk about the patient. She gave no information spontaneously, and only answered questions which the worker asked. She expressed an antagonism toward the hospital, saying she would never send any of her people there again.

From a later inquiry we learn that the patient had overt symptoms until 1935. A letter from her physician written in 1940 runs as follows: "Miss Ella H. has been a patient of mine about thirty-five years. As she has gotten older, her mentality on the whole has improved. In her young days she was a hyperthyroid case, in addition to mental peculiarities, and was operated on by Dr. F. . . . She improved somewhat, but then deteriorated again and developed the excessive bathing habits and phobias that you mention in your letter. In the last five years these have practically disappeared. . . . Her sister for the last few years has been a good deal of an invalid from arthritis, and Miss Ella H. has definitely improved in this time. She has gotten more positive in her ways of doing things and no longer ceaselessly complains. Her mentality has always been that of a child, and even that I think has markedly improved in the last four or five years."

Going through many case reports where the patients for twenty or thirty years have shown no sign of improvement, one is but too willing to take notice of a somewhat more favorable development. Yet the few facts mentioned in Dr. S.'s letter cause some doubt whether this case really belongs to the group of "contamination psychoses." A somewhat more thorough study of this case increases the doubt. Nevertheless, granting that there are cases with a more favorable development and probably milder ones evading medical attention, the group as a whole is well held together by a uniformity of development and symptomatology and at the same time clearly distinguished from the group of "compulsive killers" and from obsessives of the scrupulous type. Clinical observation and structural analysis lead to the same result. While in the compulsive group the chess game of life is played in an unorthodox way with surprising and sometimes queer moves, the rules, nevertheless, are the same followed in every other game. In the contamination group, however, a game is played where the pieces are moved in a strange fashion which clearly departs from the rules set up for a normal game.

b. ETIOLOGY AND PATHOGENESIS

There has been for some time, and still is, a strong tendency to take in every case the environmental conditions of early childhood as the decisive factor. A schizophrenic psychosis, for example, seems understandable to some as a reaction to disappointing conditions during the first years of life,—disappointing because the father was more interested in his business than in his family, while the mother was a socially ambitious woman who preferred an older, prettier sister to the patient. If this were a sufficient explanation of a schizophrenia, we should feel, I think, some embarrassment in trying to account for a development which was not schizophrenic. The conflicts on which the patients go to pieces are most frequently the same that are met always and everywhere by everyone. Therefore, one may wonder whether the conflicts create the psychotic disturbance or the incapacity to solve the average problems of life is an expression of a disease. It may be that this incapacity, by which average problems gain abnormal dimensions, is in itself the heritage of an early unsolved conflict or is an attitude acquired during the first years of life. But again we cannot tell by intuition whether peculiar early experiences which later on determine behavior in general are caused by the environment, or are early manifestations of an individual's disposition.

Determining Factors and First Manifestations

In the history of a neurotic spinster one probably will find an incestuous fixation on the father or on a brother. Reading the history with hindsight, one may proceed up to this situation as to the turning point where the direction of the future development was decided. This procedure is correct but incomplete. It might well be that the fixation was a first manifestation of a timidity which prevents a girl from leaving the protected area of the family home and trying her good or bad luck outside of this safety zone.

In a fixation on the mother, for example, the mother is not seen as another mortal woman with all her limitations, merits, and faults. She is worshipped as a divine being, raised to a height, beyond all reproach and criticism. She and all that belongs to her, things and thoughts, become absolute, objects of immutable awe and reverence. Through the mother-fixation a patient gains for himself a hold on the absolute. Infallibility is its value; but the patient has to pay for it dearly. For the mother-fixation is also an orthodox fixation on the past, which, exempted in a patient's experience from all temporal changes, is not allowed to be moved into a historical distance.

Because the patient tries to eternalize a situation which actually belongs to the past, he or she, being turned backwards, loses contact with his own time and contemporaries. It is hard to decide, in a single case, whether a patient is impeded by a mother-fixation springing from accidental conditions or is holding to the past for fear of meeting his contemporaries and of going out into the unknown.

Alice H. married at the age of twenty-seven a clergyman two years her junior. On the night of her marriage she had a dream which, many years later, she still considered to be some kind of supernatural inspiration. She dreamed that her father appeared to her and warned her against marriage, and particularly against marrying a minister. Nobody will be surprised to learn that her married life was not very happy. The patient felt unable to fulfill the duties of a minister's wife. There were constant frictions between her and her husband's family. "The patient could not adjust herself to marital sex life. . . . She had periods of extreme depressions . . . associated with feelings of weakness, inefficiency, inability to cross streets alone, panic state on riding in automobiles, and suicidal desires. . . . The patient also fretted about the possibility of her having lues; she took extreme measures to prevent infection of her children, and interpreted axillary abscesses and other symptoms as evidence of lues." During her husband's absence from home she felt much improved.

Her contamination fears were not thoroughly formulated or fixed, and she gradually relinquished them after a visit to a physician and reassurance from a Wassermann test. They still had sufficient grounds, however, for her to be anxious for another Wassermann—"if the first should have been wrong."

In her case—whatever the motives of her fear were—syphilis is a definite disease. It has an extended, but nevertheless not an unlimited, range. It can be tested, either demonstrated or excluded. It is a danger, not an omnipresent evil as it is in the case of obsessives for whom syphilis is only another name given to the nameless horror. Alice H. lived in a world the physiognomy of which was not yet basically distorted. Thus her perfectionism also was quite different from the obsessive one.

"In school she set standards of perfection for herself which she naturally never attained and was continually blaming herself for failure. She did not graduate from high school; she found the work hard and worried over it. Every spring she broke down, would miss for a few weeks, and then felt unable to accomplish the accumulated work."

This story, in which, obviously, cause and effect are interchanged, shows the patient's tendency to escape. She was always extremely sensitive. She recalled being terrified as a child when the eyes in her doll fell backward into the head. Her mother threw the doll away, and thereafter she was afraid to go to the place where the doll had been thrown, because she kept imagining its horrible eyeless appearance. One time when she heard that a murder had been committed in the neighborhood, she was restless, tense, worried, and constantly haunted with the feeling that she would in some way be blamed for this crime. From her twenty-first to her twenty-seventh year while holding a librarian's position, she was morbidly afraid of any financial transactions. In later years her sensitiveness "assumed the proportion of ideas of reference; she thought that the church people avoided her and would not speak to her because they knew of her masturbation [during adolescence] and linked it up with her attachment to her father." The patient was extremely attached to her father, a physician who had died one year before the patient's marriage. The patient devoted all her spare time to her father during his sickness, a depression which lasted for five years. She felt rather antagonistic toward her mother, "who was unusually placid and even," a statement which somewhat contradicts another one, describing the mother as a morphine addict. The father had rebelled against the church and declared himself an agnostic—an attitude which the patient admired. In an interview four years after her admission to the hospital, "she impressed the interviewer as having an exaggerated defense of her relation to her father, insisting repeatedly that it was quite normal, in spite of there being no argument or discussion concerning this; and just before she left, she pulled out of her pocket-book a time-worn newspaper clipping eulogizing her father—published at the time of his death [thirteen years ago]. She 'just wanted us to see what sort of man he was.'" The patient recognized in her own worries a replica of her father's disease.

With increasing age, when she had passed through the more dangerous zones of life, she became more and more balanced. At fifty-eight, twenty-two years after her admission, her husband reported her "in excellent health, no recurrence of her mental illness. If any of the old phobias persist, she never refers to them, and they do not interfere with her activities. She enjoys driving, has many friends, eats and sleeps well, is certainly as happy as the average person." The attachment to the father was certainly a factor which deeply influenced the patient's life before and after her marriage. However, there is little doubt that this attachment itself was not an accidental result of a family constellation, but rather an attitude—one may say—adequate to an extremely timorous girl, who "failed in all situations of any demand."

In A. G.'s case there are similar problems. A. G. in the letter to his wife reproached himself bitterly for sexual relations with a mare, with a dog, and with hens. To his physician he once denied any serious guilt feelings about these acts, which he explained as childish experimentation. If there were unconscious feelings of guilt, the question, "determing factor or early manifestation?" is not yet answered. There are good reasons to assume that these experiments were early manifestations; they express well the obsessive isolation. Hens are strange bedfellows. They will be used—even as substitutes—only by someone for whom sexual relations are not means and an expression of unification. After the intimacies with his dog, A. G. could not help thinking what might happen if the dog should give birth to monsters—"half dog, half human beings." He knew perfectly well that this was biologically impossible; he also knew that his emission went to the ground. Nevertheless, he was fascinated for a while by the idea of monstrosity, i.e., by the general theme of obsessions realized in one special form.

In the older case reports, sexual behavior or misbehavior or frustration was frequently considered to be the clue to the conflicts acted out in every neurosis. This was in accordance with the early phase of the history of psychoanalysis when sex was the paramount theme of the unconscious. Later the emphasis was shifted to aggression and hostility and the unconscious has become more and more bloodthirsty.

Let us assume for a moment that a murderous desire could be demonstrated in every case of obsession. We still should like to know why this unconscious wish manifests itself in the complex symptomatology of obsessions, a syndrome which in its multifariousness has such a well organized structure. According to Schilder, a murderous tendency is also the efficient unconscious motive of depressions. In order to avoid the specific action of killing, the depressive stops all activities.[6] This explanation not only oversimplifies; it disregards completely the very precise details of the depressive symptomatology and the course of this disease. It is up to the inventor of such hypotheses to show in regard to every single symptom how the unconscious desire has been transformed into this specific symbol, and how all the symbols together form one pathological unit. Obviously, the unconscious and the resisting forces are not free to produce arbitrarily any syndrome. In these explanations, however, the unconscious is used as a "diabolus ex machina," powerful enough to produce symptoms *ad libitum*.

The Need for Criteria

If we understand in a long sentence one vocable only, we are far from understanding the whole sentence. We do not even know what special grammatical function this one word has. In

[6] "I feel that the depressive is inhibited because he is afraid of his own aggressive impulses and does not want to act, since acting means murder." P. Schilder: *Mind, Perception, and Thought*, New York, Columbia University Press, 1942, p. 216. With permission of the publisher.

like manner, we do not know whether murderous hostility is at the bottom of obsessive behavior or is a phenomenon belonging to obsession; we do not know whether murderous hatred produces schizophrenic reactions or a schizophrenic process produces the schizophrenic murderer. As both assumptions are legitimate, we have an imperative need for criteria which permit discrimination between the various pathogenetic possibilities.

Broken families are many. Some antagonism between children and parents is the rule. Hatred is not uncommon. But schizophrenic murders are rare. The schizophrenic who kills his father probably hates him. But the hate is of a schizophrenic kind and so is the course of action followed by the schizophrenic murderer.

The psychogenetic inquiry into the biographical context alone does not provide sufficient criteria. It will always be possible to find a meaningful connection between a later and an earlier period of life. If we cannot find one, we are sure to construct one, especially if we use in our interpretations psychological equations in which two times two may have any value besides four. The actual reason for the existence of a meaningful context is the incompleteness of the single phases. Being incomplete, they can be made more complete by their relation to another phase. However, there is as a rule more than one way of completion, i.e., more than one meaningful context possible. If a child has been brought up in a puritanic environment, a perfectionist attitude on his part is understandable; but a rebellion against authority is not less understandable. There are many meaningful contexts possible because the earlier and the later phases, although completing each other, do not yet form a complete whole. In discussions about patients we frequently do not go beyond an enumeration of possibilities, some of them usually on the same level of probability. Even if we succeed in determining the factual context, we do not yet know whether the factual context represents the efficient cause.

I may illustrate this by a rough example. If we should meet in this country an American who speaks French with great ease, our curiosity would be satisfied if we learned that he has spent his childhood in France. We understand that the generic capacity to speak has been actualized and determined by certain environmental conditions. There is a positive meaningful context for an earlier and a later phase of life. We should wonder, however, if we realized that the same man who speaks beautiful French never mastered English, although he was raised in an American home and returned in his tenth year to the United States. We should search for additional reasons explaining why normally existing potentialities had not been actualized. The actual history of life never coincides with the potential one. In psychotherapy, as in all other branches of medicine, we act on the assumption that the actual history does not exhaust all potentialities. From the actual biography alone, we can never learn what other general potentialities exist or why and how, in the single case, they have been maimed. The biography reveals a positive context for an earlier and a later phase; it does not answer the question how far or why a deviation from the norm has occurred. The answers to the questions what potentialities have not been fulfilled and why they have not been fulfilled are left to the structural analysis.

Structural Analysis Confirmed by Clinical Observation

Our interest in the individual patient, our endeavors to understand his personal needs and desires, should not obscure the fact that all our therapeutical actions refer to the potentialities not of the individual but of the species. The individual is the species in its particularization. To understand the particularization—it may be a pathological case or not—we have to recur to the norm; there is no other choice. The only choice we have is that between a methodical and an unmethodical procedure, i.e., between less and more dogmatism. Structural analysis, by which the pathological disorder is comprehended as a specific distortion of the norm, can finally lead to an answer to the question how a disturbance came about. Structural analysis provides a means for the evaluation of the biographical factors. The structural analysis of obsessions has shown that the patients obsessed by the fear of contamination live in a basically distorted world. The disturbance is not limited to the interpersonal relations. Obsession is no primary disorder of the historico-social sphere of a person. Evil, death, and decay, are experienced as cosmic substances and powers; the evil is not experienced as a theme of social institutions or as a moral problem, either as command or interdiction, but as "being"—as a metaphysical reality. Because these patients are put under the ban of a cosmic power, they are less free than the compulsive killers who resist a moral law. The patients do not have the freedom of action assumed by Freud and Binswanger in their conversation quoted at the beginning of this paper. Their failure is not due to a "lack of spirituality," but to the violence which they suffer in the physiognomic sphere, i.e., in the realm of their vital, not their spiritual, existences. A psychogenic origin of such a basic change is very improbable. The refractoriness to psychotherapy supports this assumption. In comparison with the favorable results in the group of "compulsive killers"—as in H. C. F.'s case—the lack of success in contamination cases is still more striking. Experiences gained with one of the two groups must, therefore, not be generalized—or applied to the other one.

The secondary gain to the obsessive is small. The fact that an obsessive patient dominates the family scene proves very little. Similar conditions prevail in a case of carcinoma or of a tuberculosis—in practically any severe disease as long as the patients remain in their family homes. An obsessive may use his rituals to enslave mother or brother or sister. But the use he makes of his disturbances does not prove that this, as a "causa finalis," produces or maintains the disturbance. Certainly those patients who practice their rituals later in complete solitude and concealment have not even a chance for any such secondary gains.

The family situations show no typical pattern. There are nagging and meticulous mothers, but also others tolerant, patient, amiable; there are austere fathers, but also others indulgent and lenient; there are alcoholics, but also others with poise and self-control. There are large and small families, with many or few brothers and sisters; some of the patients were only children; some of them were wanted, some of them not. In some cases early sexual experiences are mentioned; in others they are denied; where they occurred they were not different from those experienced by many people who never showed any serious neurotic disturbances. Childbirth is quite frequently noted as preceding more dramatic manifestations of obsessive symptoms. It may be that the incidence of early death of one of the parents and interference of aunts in the education exceeds expectations somewhat in this group. There are quite a few broken homes; but the broken home which creates a disastrous atmosphere for a child is, perhaps, at the same time the expression of a hereditary constellation.

Family Situation and Hereditary Constellation

Reports of social workers, who visited Frances U., admitted to the hospital in 1913, give a striking picture of the weird home from which this patient came, and of the family from which she sprang.

The first report, dated November 20, 1921, runs as follows:

"The home was visited twice last week in the afternoon. The house is the largest on the street, but gives one the impression of an institution rather than a home. On both visits a grim looking old lady, the patient's aunt, opened the door. She said the patient is perfectly well and goes out every day . . . not on business, but on pleasure. . . . She has a great deal to do and has no time for visitors; possibly she may see visitor if she will call next week."

"A third visit was made this morning. An old woman, as stern and forbidding looking as the aunt, admits visitor. She states that she is the patient's mother. The patient is upstairs busy with 'receipts and clerical work' and can't be disturbed. 'She is perfectly well and goes away every summer and tends to all our business' and 'the family does not care for her to see the doctor.' Visitor is politely shown the door."

A second inquiry was made in 1938:

"The bell was not answered. The house has all the appearances of having been vacant for a long time. . . . The neighbor, a woman of 29 who had always lived next door, told visitor that the patient's two aunts had died many years ago and the mother died five years ago. The brother and the patient lived alone in the very large house until death of patient two years ago following a stroke. The family were known to be very wealthy, owning considerable property and ground rents. They owned most of the property in the neighborhood. The old ladies, patient, and brother kept strictly to themselves—they barely condescended to bow—the whole lot were considered proud, queer, and aloof, and living only for each other. They have never been known to have any help in the house. The patient used to be seen going out and returning with provisions. She was regarded as 'crazy' in the neighborhood. She had 'yelling spells'—had been known to stand on front steps and scream. Several years ago she was taken in an ambulance, but soon returned. Neighborhood gossip had it she was taken to Maryland General Hospital and 'was so crazy they wouldn't keep her.' The brother is supposed to be living alone, at least it is thought he sleeps there at night. Even when the patient was bedridden in her last illness the brother took care of her and engaged no outside help."

Back in 1913, during the first weeks of Frances' treatment her case looked as if it fitted very well in the anticipated scheme. Her father and mother had been separated when the patient was a year old, and patient had never seen her father since. She was the younger of two children and very much attached to her brother, two years her senior. She revealed her hatred for her maiden aunts, whose jealous affection she resented. Throughout childhood she was much restricted by their prudish, repressive attitude. Nevertheless, she showed affection to them because she feared that the aunts might otherwise leave their money to charity. One of the aunts had tuberculosis. The patient had been warned never to shock the aunt, yet one day when she saw a cat run over by a car and killed, she rushed first to this aunt and told her the frightening story. The next morning the aunt had a hemorrhage. The patient saw blood in a china basin. She suddenly felt that there was blood on everything, but especially on her hands. Thus the hand-washing started. "I was to blame for the hemorrhage without knowing it and washed my hands because of this sense of guilt." This happened when Frances was twenty-eight years old, four years before her admission. The record does not say whether or not Frances saw herself in a role of a Lady Macbeth. Anyway, it gradually became apparent that her obsessions had begun much earlier. "At about twelve the patient had the obsession to touch objects she passed when in the house, but not at other places. It was especially the doors in the parlor on the first floor. She frequently had to come downstairs at night to touch these doors before going to bed.'Something seemed to tell me I had to touch the doors and wall'. . . . This continued for four years without change. When studying she also had to turn back a page and read the last three lines over three times. . . . At sixteen, she began to have to sew things three or five times. This continued until she was twenty-seven, gradually becoming worse, until she could not sew at all. At twenty-seven, she had to make the right side of clothes larger than the left and take more stitches. . . . Then she began to buy three or five of all small objects, e.g., gloves, handkerchiefs, powder, etc. This continued until she was thirty-one, when the fear of tuberculosis began. . . . After the aunt's hemorrhage the patient would wash her hands in rapid succession. After touching anything she would wash them. Thus the patient was washing her hands most of the time. In a week she began to wash her gloves and shoes, in fact everything. She kept a list of the things she must wash. This continued for two years without a change."

Two years before her admission the aunts returned from a vacation and brought her a hat-pin, breast-pin, and a dress. "The hat-pin was in a traveling medicine case with the throat sprayer of the aunt. The hat-pin was wrapped in white paper which was moistened with the fluid from the sprayer. When she touched it it was a shock to her. . . . She carried it upstairs and wrapped it in paper and hid it in a back room, where it remained for two months. She washed her hands in *pure carbolic acid*, getting a severe burn. . . . She tried to buy a similar hat-pin, but couldn't. Finally she took off the outer paper with her hands, then cut off the head of the pin without taking off the original paper. She picked up the head of the pin with the scissors and dropped it in pure carbolic acid, and threw away the scissors. Then she put it away, taking it in her hand, but could hardly hold it and washed repeatedly afterwards. She finally sewed the head of the pin on a hat. She felt perfectly terrible when she wore the hat. A year later she did away with the pin.

In April 1912 (half a year later) she went out walking in a park. She stepped on some sputum. On returning, a girl friend told her that the man living in the house in front of which she had stepped on the sputum had tuberculosis. From this she got the fear of tuberculosis. She touched nothing in her room, but took off in her room the clothes she wore that day. She threw away much valuable clothing and jewelry. She remained in her room for two weeks in a hysterical crying condition.

Frances was never very consistent in her own explanation of her obsessions, relating, for example, her number ritual at one time to the family situation, at another time to the shape of male genitalia. One could never say which of her explanations was the last and definite one. Perhaps there was some truth in all the references which she mentioned.

Sex played a paramount role, but sex in the queer form which her theories of procreation reveal. According to her, "she knew nothing of sexual matters until about fifteen, when the girls at school told of how children were born and of intercourse by the insertion of the male organ. She was disgusted at this and never really believed it. . . . She always believed until present (referring to the age of thirty-two) that a girl lost her virtue if she inserted anything, a syringe, in the vagina." Another time she said that "from sixteen to seventeen she thought that if a man and a woman slept in the same bed the woman would become pregnant. After seventeen she did not believe this, but thought intercourse occurred but once. Intercourse consisted of just touching the genitalia. . . . When she heard someone say that a child was some blood relation to him . . . she evolved the idea that *in the sexual act blood passed from the male to the female.* She also thought that blood might be the seminal fluid. This idea persisted until 1911 (age twenty-nine) when she heard a person say that the white of an egg increased a man's sexual desire. From this she evolved the idea that *semen must be like the white of an egg.* Mucoid *sputum* which resembles the white of an egg must, therefore, resemble semen." All these contradictory statements about sexual relations have some traits in common: pollution, artificiality, violence, distance.

Frances had a fatuous love for the doctor of her aunt. But she avoided him pointedly. "When told the doctor was coming she dressed and went out—'although I would have loved to have talked to him.' " At the age of nineteen she dreamed of a wedding trip with a lawyer whom she had met at church. . . "He persisted in getting one room. I was fighting against this and told him if we had separate rooms my love would be more lasting, that I never approved of that. . . . I gave in to him, but I sat up all night and I was unhappy and miserable. . . . I woke while arguing with him. On awaking I felt I did not care for him any more."

"She would never expose herself to others. She always thought she would lose all affection for anyone if she saw them partly clothed." "She told her brother that if she ever saw him in a bathing suit she would not care for him any more."

It has frequently been emphasized that "the compulsion neurotics are, as a rule, superior persons who are striving with tremendous energy to attain to higher things. . . . The neurosis arises as . . . an expression of the essentially moral qualities of the patient, that is, those qualities which insist upon continuing the fight for further advance on the road to development."[7] It is hard, however, in many cases to discover anything of these superior moral qualities. It seems to me that the obsessive patients instead of fighting for further advance on the road to development live and fight on a level below the normal sympathetic relations. Their prudishness is not an expression of their strict moral demands, of their modesty and chastity. They have lost all natural naivete. They do not protect their intimate life against obtrusive views. All that belongs to sex and corporality appears to them disfigured and misshapen; it appears as something awful.

From a book Frances learned the differences of sex. From that time on she was anxious to see the reality. She went to a Turkish bath. "The first time she became sick; she was so shocked, because for the first time in her life she saw a woman naked. She continued the baths, but would never expose herself or go in the pool when anyone else was there. . . . Before this experience she thought that women were not all alike." She mentioned this idea several times. One day she handed the doctor a note on which "she indicated her idea in the usual veiled manner—'just one of my thoughts. I wondered if some had nothing at all. The same with the opposite sex.' "

Whatever page we turn in this case history, everywhere we find the same queer, morbid, attitude, the same chaotic notions of the world. The home situation, a house without a father, but with two maiden aunts, an unmarried brother, a "stern and forbidden looking mother", were not propitious. However, it seems to me the problems caused by the involved situation did not create Frances's troubles, but her innate character created the problems in relation, of course, to the material offered by the environment.

The Physiognomy of the Obsessive World, Compared with that of Hashish Intoxication

Obsessive experience of this type presents precisely the reverse of the conditions caused by "sympathy poisons", like alcohol or

[7] S. E. Jelliffe and W. A. White: *Diseases of the Nervous System*, Lea and Febiger, Philadelphia, 1935, p. 929-930. With permission of the publisher.

hashish. A few quotations from Baudelaire's essay on hashish intoxication will show the striking contrasts. Baudelaire called his essay "Le poème du haschisch." The accuracy of Baudelaire's observations has been confirmed by recent experimental work; the beauty, clarity, and profundity of his presentation have never been excelled. Turning to an imaginary novice Baudelaire says:[8] "I assume that you have been prudent enough to choose well the right moment for this adventurous expedition. Every perfect debauch demands perfect leisure. You know that hashish produces a diversification not only of the individual, but also of the environment, of the milieu. You have no duties which demand punctuality or accuracy—no domestic worries—no amorous complaints." Thus the keynote of this inebriety is given as leisure, repose, abandonment. "The first signs: . . . you are overwhelmed by a certain hilarity, absurd perhaps, but irresistible. . . . The simplest words, the most trivial ideas, show a bizarre and new physiognomy. You will be amazed that heretofore you have found them so simple. . . . Among the emotions caused by hashish, humaneness plays a rather important role; some soft, indolent, silent benevolence. . . . Indeed, during this phase of the intoxication a new refinement and increased acuteness of all senses occur. Smell, sight, touch, audition, all share equally in this enhancement. The eyes see the infinite. The ears hear almost imperceptible tones in the midst of the loudest tumult. . . . Sometimes it happens that the individuality vanishes and that that objectivity, proper to pantheistic poets, will be revealed in you to such an abnormal degree that looking upon the objects of the external world you will forget yourself and you will soon flow over into them. Your view is fixed upon a tree which is bent harmoniously by the wind. . . . You will ascribe to the tree your passions, your longing, your melancholy; its sighs and oscillations will become yours, and soon you will be the tree. . . . You know that hashish all the time produces marvellous phenomena of light, a glorious lustre, cascades of melted gold. . . . Hashish spreads over all life like a mysterious, miraculous varnish. Hashish gives to it solemn shades of colors and illuminates it into its last depths. . . . With one word, everything,

[8]C. L. Baudelaire: *Les Paradis Artificiels*, (my translation).

the universe of beings, appears to you in a new splendor you have never dreamed of. Grammar, even the arid grammar, is turned into something like a charming spell, which awakens the words and embodies them in bones and flesh. . . . Music, the second language, speaks to you about yourself and tells you the legend of your life. It is embodied in you, and you are completely drawn into it. . . . I think I said enough about the immense growth of time and space, two ideas always connected with each other. I also said that one visualizes this without sadness or fear. With a tint of a joyful melancholy the mind looks through the depth of years and embarks boldly on borderless perspectives. . . . Harmony, the equilibrium of lines, the beautiful rhythms of motions, appear to the dreamer as necessities, one could well say as *duties*, obliging not only all other creatures, but also the dreamer, who, in this phase of the crisis, finds himself mysteriously endowed with the power of perceiving the infinite rhythms of the universe."

Conclusion; Physiognomic Changes as Criterion

The hilarity, the humaneness, the intensification and beauty of sensory impressions, the music, the harmony, the fading of boundaries between subject and object, all this is in such a sharp and direct contrast with obsessions that we cannot but see there two extremes of human existence, both equally remote from the norm and in that respect both belonging to each other. As we know that one of them is caused by a poison, we do not hesitate to assume that some similar conditions exist for the other one too. The next conclusion is that wherever we find a basic change in the physiognomy of the world and accordingly in our relation to it, there we are confronted with a psychosis, a disease which seizes man; there we are confronted with a change in the mode of existence which befalls man, to which he reacts, but which he neither consciously nor unconsciously produces.

C. "ANLAGEN" AND CONFLICT IN OBSESSIONS

This still leaves two extreme possibilities: one is that obsessions are the manifestations of a fatal "anlage", unescapable manifestations, whatever the milieu might be; the other is that obsessions are caused by and related to environmental conditions also. But there are many other possibilities between the two extremes. We know people who will become neurotic only under extreme difficulties, and others who will develop without neurotic symptoms only under unusually favorable conditions. There are some who are able to deal with many adverse circumstances, and others who collapse when confronted with the average problems of life.

Bertha L.'s father was a junk dealer. The family situation could not help to build up the patient's self-assertion. She daydreamed of wealth and splendor, at times imagining that she was an adopted child and that some time illustrious parents would be discovered. The business of a junk dealer has no social prestige; it is a dirty business, a fact which probably was one determining factor in the patient's life and sickness. However, her brothers and sisters, who grew up under the same conditions, did not become obsessive. We may add that in the report of the social worker, the house in which Bertha's family lived was described as "small but comfortable looking and well located." The effects of the environment depend on the existing "anlagen."

It seems to me one would expect some proportion, not only between conditions and neurosis in general, but between the specific conditions and the specific kind of disturbances.

Considering structural analysis and clinical experience, a psychogenic etiology seems very improbable. Even if it should not be possible to exclude it completely, two things at least are assured: a different pathogenesis between the group of "compulsive killers" and that of contamination obsessions, and a "functional autonomy" of the disease in the latter group. Even if the obsession springs from a conflict, it does not remain centered around it. It is quite possible that an "anlage" does not need to manifest itself under all conditions; an additional environmental factor may be necessary. It seems equally difficult to prove or to reject this possibility.

Binder,[9] in an excellent study about the relation of crimes and obsessions, distinguishes psychogenic and organic cases of ob-

[9]H. Binder: Zwang und Kriminalität, *Schweizer Archiv für Neurologie und Psychiatrie*, Vol. 54, 1944. pp. 31-68 and pp. 301-329; vol. 55, 1945. pp. 4-15.

sessions. He subdivides the psychogenic group into two subgroups. For the one he assumes a definite, abnormal "Persönlichkeits-anlage." In this group the milieu is of secondary importance. He speaks of a psychopathic, anakastic form of obsessive development. In the other group the milieu is the decisive factor. Although a specific, sensitive "anlage" is not lacking, it still may be in the realm of normal variations. In both groups Binder sees obsessions as reactions to conflicts. In the first one, the "anlage" leads with a certain degree of fatal necessity to those conflicts which end in obsessions. It seems to me, however, that any conflict would bring the "anlagen" to their own development. But even if this additional psychogenic factor is indispensable, the obsession is not the pseudo-solution of this conflict. The theme of the obsession has only a loose connection with the provoking conflict. This would explain why an obsession once started remains so resistant to psychotherapy. After all, most probably it is a disease—a destruction—within the realm of drives, within the "Id" itself, to use Freud's terminology.

In a discussion of manic-depressive states Freud said: "A factor, probably somatic in origin, not to be explained psychogenetically, manifests itself in the regular alleviation of symptoms in the evening. Here the question arises whether an Ego-privation (purely narcissistic Ego-insult) is not *in itself* sufficient to produce the phenomenon of melancholia, and whether a toxic impoverishment of Ego-libido could not directly result in certain forms of the disease."[10]

Obsessions and Sadism

In regard to obsessions, Freud did not admit this possibility. The psychological conflict and regression to the anal-sadistic level were assumed to be the decisive factors. Yet R. Brun, who sticks closely to the lines of orthodox psychoanalysis, insists that the extreme forms of obsessions grow only in the ground of innate constitutional "anlagen."[11] "Whoever does not have these

[10]S. Freud: "Trauer und Melancholie" in *Zur Technik der Psychoanalyse und zur Metapsychologie,* Internat. psa. Verlag, Vienna, 1924, p. 269.

[11]R. Brun: *Allgemeine Neurosenlehre,* B. Schwabe & Co., Bale, 1942, p. 366 ff.

'anlagen' cannot become an obsessive." Brun thinks that the "anlagen" are characterized by "a constitutional intensification of emotional ambivalence" and by "an unusually strong sadism." This interpretation leads to the question whether and to what extent the experience and behavior of children during the so-called anal-sadistic phase coincide with the disgust and sadism met in later periods of life.

For the child, dirt does not yet have the physiognomy of decay, i.e., the physiognomy which torments the obsessive. The psychoanalytical answer to this argument is that during the anal-sadistic period the barriers of shame and disgust have not yet been erected. But only through its physiognomy is something an object for a drive. The repelling physiognomy removed, dirt is not yet or no longer dirt; for dirt is not a thing plus the stamp of a prohibiting taboo. A baby who plays with its excrement does not touch dirt, just as its aggressions are not sadistic.

Freud used patterns of adult conduct in order to interpret the behavior of children. And he did this by not discriminating the striking differences and by disregarding the essential characteristics of such sexual attitudes as sadism. Freud explains sadism as "that general drive for overpowering, which we call sadism, whenever we find it in the service of the sexual function." Here we get the impression that sadism in its pure form, as in the case of lust murder, is nothing but the intensification and, perhaps, isolation of a normal drive. "It also has to give important aid during the fully matured, normal, sexual life."[12] Certainly in normal sexual life a man wants to gain and conquer a woman. But here conquest means that she gives herself spontaneously and voluntarily to him, that he is desired and accepted by her. In other words, the conquest is not against the will of the conquered. The conquered is respected, is esteemed as a person who could also deny herself. Without the possibility of refusal, the acceptance would lose all its meaning; the woman would be no partner, no You who answers my calling. The sadist, however, is not willing to tolerate refusal and to subject himself to the choice of the other; he uses violence, but not as a means for

[12]S. Freud: "Die Disposition zur Zwangsneurose," *Schriften zur Neurosenlehre*, Internat. psa. Verlag, Vienna, 1931, p. 11-12.

sexual intercourse, as in rape. The sadist enjoys violence as such. To chain the victim, to expose her, to shame her, to torment her, to defile her, perhaps to kill her—these are the sadistic intentions. The chaining expresses the fact that the victim has ceased to be a person, has been transformed into a thing. In normal sexual life a man is inclined to idolize his partner; the more beautiful, the more charming, she is, the more blessed will he be through her choice. Yet the sadist enjoys vitiating her, forcing sex upon her as excretion and dirt; he is thrilled by the mutilation and degradation of beauty. The sadist does not need to do all these acts himself; it suffices for him to remain a spectator and to have all the tormenting done by a third person. The sadist does not enter into the relation of a partnership; his enjoyment is to throw the other one out of existence as a partner, a person, an individual—as a living being. The sadist is incapable of entering into a "We"-group. One may call the sadistic domination of a victim mastery, but this mastery, its procedures, and the objects of its conquest, are radically different from the common instinct of mastery displayed in normal sexual life. A sadist may have intercourse with the woman he has chained, beaten, and polluted, but this "object" of his libido is not the same woman any longer that she was before the beating, not the "object" a man desires in normal sexual life. Sadism is not the direct continuation of normal hostility and aggression. The little jokes of biting and beating which occur in sexual relations have nothing to do with sadism. The external events count very little. The meaning of actions cannot be detached from their relation to values, from the intention of a realization, preservation, increase, or annihilation of values. When in summertime we kill flies, we do it because they annoy us and because we see them as vermin, which have no value of their own and, therefore, no right to exist. Vermin is a concept of zoological evaluation. It certainly is anthropocentric. Nevertheless, this evaluation removes for us the shade of cruelty from our action. Cruel is the man who violates, ignoring or disregarding, the "inalienable" values or rights which he should see and regard. The sadist does not overlook these inalienable rights. He has a keen eye for them; he focuses his own interest and fixes the attention of his victim on them, but only in order to destroy them with explicit consciousness. The sadist hates, yet he does not hate the odious but rather the charming for its charms. Sadism is a real perversion; for the destruction of values which are clearly felt, the destruction of these values against their intrinsic demand to be cherished and preserved, is the core of the sadistic enjoyment.

Freud's Reversal of Norm and Pathology

In deciding that sadism was a variety of the common drive of mastery, Freud accomplished the feat of explaining a pathological, morbid condition as a normal phase in early life history. This in turn enabled him and his followers to explain disturbances as the result of a conflict between normal, usual desires and their undesired control. In normalizing the morbid, it becomes possible to "pathologize" the norm, yet not without several other presuppositions. One of them, as has been said, is that the individual is a being locked up in himself. Each man is an isolated organism, which, using things as mere objects for satisfaction of its drives, finds this goal in certain states of the body. "We are not interested by what genital practices people gain their lust as long as it does not endanger their security."[13] It seems to me that with this view autism has become the principle of psychological explanation. Indeed, if the goal of sexual desire is the lust, the perception of orgasm, the means of reaching this goal are of no great importance. In this case our only concern may be whether or not the self-respect of our patients "is strong and healthy enough to stand the necessity of secretiveness, the possible threat of ostracism from society, in case their sources of lust are different from the socially accepted ones."[13] But if the goal of sexual desire is the unification with a partner, if orgasm accompanies unification, sexual practices clearly express the actual relations of a person to the world, to other human beings, and to himself. If a woman is only an object for the satisfaction of libido, it does not matter whether she is a chained and beaten body or a person who can give herself. The terminology, "object of libido," substitutes for the person,

[13]Frida Fromm-Reichman in a lecture: "Intensive Psychotherapy of a Catatonic Girl", delivered to the Maryland Psychiatric Association, Nov. 21, 1944.

who in her experience is directed to the world, impersonal drives, which have no direction towards the world.[14] While a person on the one hand exists in an I-world, in an I-You relation, i.e., in a relation of mutual completion, drives, on the other hand, are centered in themselves. Although frequently personified, they are blind, without approach to the other, and without meaningful contact with the world. They are closed in within the huge bag of the "Id." One may well wonder whether the term, "objects of libido," does not represent a theory of reduction which takes the mutilation for the norm.

Because man is an isolated organism, therefore—this is the second presupposition—, his primary interests do not reach beyond his skin, certainly not beyond the horizon of his senses. Consequently, the reality which expands beyond this horizon is a purely negative factor. It prevents the direct satisfaction of drives; it is also an obstacle in the satisfaction of the anal-sadistic instincts, and thereby a cause of obsessions.

Ambiguity of the Term "Meaningful"

As the drives supposedly have their own existence and as the "Ego", which entertains some scanty relations with the world, is only a vassal of the "Id," the word "meaningful" has become a very ambiguous term. The constitution of any behavior seems to be sufficiently explored if its expediency for a drive has been established. Its importance for the I-world relation matters very little. Attitudes and conditions that appear meaningful in relation to the satisfaction of a drive need not be meaningful as far as the relation of a person to the world is concerned. In fact, they usually are not; for everything that is meaningful for a man in so far as he is a "citizen" seems to antagonize the immediate satisfaction of a drive. The satisfaction of a drive is an end in itself. At this point the chain of meaningful contexts suddenly breaks down; it does not reach beyond this ultimate goal. The Freudian interpretation of a meaningful action, therefore, is at least indifferent to its effects upon man as a member of the human world. An action will be called meaningful as long as it is supposed to serve a drive, however

[14]Cp. R. Allers: *The Successful Error*, Sheed and Ward, New York, 1940, p. 111.

destructive—and therefore opposed to meaning—it might be in the sphere of social, ethical, and historical existence. The word "meaningful" has become the name of an irrational principle. As long as we are not aware of this paradoxical situation, all efforts to reach a common basis of discussion will be frustrated.

Human Needs; Their Relative Power and Urgency

In recent years, "needs" have dislodged the "drives." This change, in spite of the vagueness of the term "need," borrowed from economics and everyday-life usage, could have been a decisive step forward. If we speak about needs, we speak, by implication, about man who is in need of this and that. Needs do not exist independently, side by side, each one of them a little sovereign, like the drives in Freud's conception. Needs imply relations of man to the world. Man in his needs is directed to the world. The drives were centered in themselves. When we think about needs instead of drives, we turn our consideration from an organism isolated within the world to a person in relation to the world. It is man, as an undivided person, who has many various needs. In abstraction, we can analyze the unity of the manifold needs and deal with one of them separately. But we should not forget that all together they form a whole, and that every one of them has its function as a part of this whole. This whole has a structure marked by the relative urgency of the single needs.

Unfortunately, we continue to speak about needs in the plural, as if every one of them existed by itself alone. Yet if by an obsessive ritual or by a schizophrenic withdrawal a need should be satisfied, the question remains: why does the need to lead a "reasonable" and meaningful life permit being completely dissatisfied? If a lifetime spent in the fight against contamination means satisfaction of a need, we still wonder whether a need which gains satisfaction from this distressing behavior is not a pathological need. A need which permits or requires a pathological satisfaction is—most probably—a pathological need. The quantities of water drunk by a patient suffering from *diabetes insipidus* satisfy a need, but a need determined by pathological conditions.

When we compare an obsessive individual with a normal one, we cannot overlook the fact that the structure of the whole and the relative urgency of the different needs have been deeply altered. Whatever need is satisfied by obsessive behavior, obviously it paralyzes the satisfaction of other needs. A part has emancipated itself from the whole and grows at the expense of the rest—like a carcinoma. The assumed satisfaction of one need does not explain the structural alteration of the totality of needs. In the case of the "compulsive killers" we find an integer structure of the whole; in the case of a contamination-obsession, we find the structure of the whole distorted.

When we speak—in the plural—about needs and their satisfaction we will quickly reach the point where we again treat the needs as sovereign entities. Words do not simply verbalize ideas we clearly had before the verbalization took place. Terms have a dynamics of their own which interferes not only with the formulation but also with the formation of our thoughts. The usage of the term "needs" can hardly be separated from a "mosaic-theory," the inadequateness of which has been proven by "Gestalt psychology." The theoretical solution of our problem is, therefore, not to discuss individual needs, but man in the various aspects of his needs, i.e., man in his manifold relations to the world,—to nature as well as to history, to other men, and to himself. Our understanding of psychopathology depends on a preceding analysis of the norm of human existence and of man's needs in their totality, their theme, their structure, and their changing or lasting relative urgency and power.

Recourse to the Norm is Peremptory

The opposite method, to hit upon the norm by studying pathological cases, has become in this century the paramount style of interpreting human existence. Consciousness is understood from the unconscious, waking life from sleep, insight from dream, order from chaos. Picasso paints the chaos, Joyce writes in a language of dreams, Lawrence hails the unconscious, because they are all convinced that the chaos, the dream, the unconscious, are at the very bottom of things. The method of conjecturing the norm from pathological disturbances is not a technique chosen for its handiness; it echoes metaphysical tenets. The method is justified only if sleep, dream, the unconscious, the Id, are *more real* than the Ego, which exists as the saprophyte of the Id, sometimes as a harmless sponger, at other times as a destructive parasite. This metaphysics creates a paradoxical situation. Everything set down as truly positive can only be expressed by negative words and concepts. The un-conscious is a negation of the conscious, the impersonal "Id" the negation of personal existence. When awake we can explore dreams, but dreams do not comprehend awakeness. It is true that in some mythologies Night brings forth Light; yet we will never understand light as a shade of darkness. The method which hits upon the norm by studying pathological cases is based on a peculiar displacement of norm and morbidity.

The theme of psychiatry is different from that of all other branches of medicine. While they are concerned—primarily or exclusively—with man as a living being, an organism, psychiatry deals also with man as a citizen of the human world. Our understanding of psychopathological problems depends on a preceding interpretation of man in his role as a citizen. The interpretation accepted in our epoch by a great majority comes from a psychiatrist, Freud, but it does not have its origin in psychiatry; it is a philosophy, very similar to that of Thomas Hobbes. For both philosophers man is a citizen in spite of himself. He accepts citizenship as a compromise in order to escape from the evils connected with the state of nature. Even so "the discomfort in civilization" prevails. However, as a thinking being, man has always broken through the horizon of sensory experience, the horizon of drives, and their satisfaction. This break-through creates new "needs," which neither originate within the realm of drives, nor gain their energy from them, nor find their satisfaction in them, nor are secondary or negligible in comparison with them.

In Freud's dichotomy, man's relations to the human world are negative, secondary and conventional, while the drives are positive, original and natural. That they are natural is their main qualification. All other qualifications, therefore, are forced upon them by conventional evaluations. Among the drives one is as natural as the other. This indifference towards values prevents even a distinction between normal and morbid. Disturbances—so it seems—can only arise from a conflict between the conventional, inhibitory forces and the natural tendencies. However, if man's relations to the human world are not purely negative and conventional, but meaningful in themselves, a disturbance which prevents the fulfillment of these needs may well have its origin in a disease, or a defect, within the realm of the drives.

Freud never gave up exploring and formulating the presuppositions on which his work was based. Neither all his followers nor all his opponents are equally aware of the many assumptions implied by the so-called empirical observation of facts. In psychiatry, where biological, psychological, and anthropological problems meet, the number of concealed hypotheses is particularly large. Even in a discussion of a special theme, therefore, we cannot dispense with the reexamination of the general basic assumptions. A recourse to the norm is imperative. This implies, as we have seen, a change in method as well as in matter. In method: from the genetic-biographical approach to structural analysis; in matter: from a study of man as an isolated organism to a consideration of man in his manifold relations to the world. In applying these principles to the problem of obsessions we have been able, starting from an analysis of disgust, to outline the destruction which befalls the I-world relations and completely reverses the physiognomy of the world in that disease. We then could show how the symptomatology in its manifold details is shaped by the basic change of the sympathetic relations. This enabled us to discriminate between the psychotic and the neurotic forms of obsessions and to establish a general psychological criterion for this universally important distinction.